6756

W9-DAM-550

DATE DUE

DEMCO 38-297

BELLOC, THE MAN

Hilaire Belloc by Eric Gill (1910)

BELLOC, THE MAN

by

Eleanor and Reginald Jebb

THE NEWMAN PRESS

Westminster, Maryland

1957

First published in 1956
This edition printed 1957

Library of Congress Catalog Card Number : 57-6692

PRINTED AND BOUND IN GREAT BRITAIN BY
BUTLER AND TANNER LTD, FROME AND LONDON

FOR

MARIANNE, PHILIP, ANTHONY

AND JULIAN

WITH LOVE FROM M. AND D.

Contents

Illustrations

Foreword

THE two parts of this testimony to Hilaire Belloc approach
their subject from different angles. My wife has recorded a
continuous series of memories from her earliest childhood
up to 1914 when, with the death of her mother, the outbreak of
the first world war, and the beginning of her own school days away
from home, her father's life—and indeed that of King's Land—under-
went great changes. My own contribution consists of a number of
somewhat disjointed essays, in which I have tried to show some of
the characteristics of the man and his work that have impressed me
during the years that I have known him.

Though perhaps the form of the book is unusual, divided, as it is,
into two quite unconnected parts, we hope that the general picture
that emerges may help to throw some light on the unique qualities
and many-sided genius of one whom so many have admired and
loved without even having seen him.

Both of us fully realize the inadequacy of our testimony, but if it
helps to fill in some gaps in the memory or the knowledge of those
who read it, it will have served its purpose. To mirror in words the
whole Belloc would be an impossible task, yet the random impressions
of those who knew him intimately may serve to enlighten others less
fortunate. That is what we have both tried to give, and it has been a
labour of love.

I should like to acknowledge with thanks Messrs Gerald Duckworth's
permission to reproduce in Chapter 8 a few lines from the introduction
I wrote to their latest edition of Belloc's *Sonnets and Verse*, and a number
of quotations from his poems in that volume. I am also grateful to
the Editor of *Blackfriars* for allowing me to quote a passage from an
article I wrote for that paper many years ago; to Mrs Gill and Messrs
Williams and Norgate for leave to include a sketch of Belloc drawn by
Eric Gill which appeared in the *French Revolution*; and to Mr Allen

Chappelow for permission to use his photograph of the dining-room at King's Land.

My special thanks are due to Mr Stanley Scott for the trouble he took in bringing to my notice and photographing the Gill picture, and to Mr Sagar, who so kindly lent me his valuable, and as yet unpublished, account of the Marconi affair, which was of great assistance to me. I am indebted to him, too, for the advice he gave me on certain points in other chapters.

REGINALD JEBB

PART I

THE MAN AND HIS WORK

by Reginald Jebb

1 *Introductions and Background*

THE first time I met Belloc was in 1921. I had recently come back from the first world war and was in partnership in a preparatory school in Horsham. I shall not easily forget the impression that first meeting made upon me. I had read, as most people had read, a certain number of his books, and, like almost every officer in the British Army, had devoured with interest what he had to say in *Land and Water* about the progress of the war, but I had little or no knowledge then of the man himself or of the varied experiences of his life.

What struck me most as the door opened and he came quickly in was the squareness of the figure in front of me. The straight horizontal line of his broad shoulders formed the top of a squat parallelogram of which the sides and lower end were supplied by a vast overcoat, unbuttoned and falling in straight lines almost to his ankles. Above it was the almost perfect square of his head and even what could be seen of the wide black trousers that appeared below the overcoat suggested the lower ends of two additional, more elongated, parallelograms. He had come intent upon a single purpose: in a few days he was due to go sailing in the *Nona*, and one of his crew had failed him. He had heard that I had done some sailing and asked Eleanor, his daughter, to bring him over to see if I could fill the vacant place. Alas! in spite of his determination, his mission came to nothing. My school term had started and I could not leave, and indeed I should have been of little help on the high seas, as my only experience of sailing had been two lazy holidays on the Norfolk Broads. The visit was a short one, and I remember no more of it. He was gone as quickly and as suddenly as he had appeared, presumably to continue his quest.

During the rest of that year I saw him, as far as I can remember, only once. I had brought Eleanor from Horsham to King's Land on the back of my motor-bicycle. He met us in the dining-room and at once offered me red wine of his own bottling. He had no recollection, I

3

feel sure, of having seen me before, and indeed it was not until after I had become engaged to Eleanor in 1922 that our occasional meetings were for him anything more than first introductions to a stranger he was never likely to meet again. At King's Land that day, in the stone-flagged, fourteenth-century dining-room, there was no sign of the impetuous vigour and purpose that had struck me so much before. He was the courteous, slightly aloof Victorian host, offering hospitality to one whom his daughter had introduced.

Later I was to experience many other sides of his character and to piece together bit by bit an outline of the full tumultuous life that his energy and genius had fashioned. For the purpose of this record I propose to reverse the process, setting out first of all the main incidents of his life and thereafter against that background, offering my testimony to some of his many qualities and achievements.

Belloc was born in 1870 in the village of La Celle St Cloud twelve miles from Paris. His mother, the daughter of Joseph Parkes who had made a name for himself in preparing the way for the Reform Bill of 1832, was in her forty-first year when he was born. She was a woman of strong character and pronounced tastes, and the vitality that gave her a child at so mature an age and remained with her till her ninety-fourth year was phenomenal. Brought up as a Unitarian in Birmingham among people of intelligence and great mental activity (her mother was the granddaughter of Joseph Priestley, the scientist) she decided, after a visit to Ireland in 1864, to become a Catholic, a step which so astounded her father that he had grave fears for her sanity. In 1867 she married a French barrister, Louis Belloc, who was the son of Hilaire Belloc, an artist of considerable fame. During her married life, and for some years after the death of her husband in 1872, she divided her time between the house at La Celle and her mother's in London, and numbered among her friends and acquaintances many famous people in both countries. Thus she continued to move in a society of culture and ideas similar to, but of greater range than, that in which she had been brought up.

Her husband, Louis Belloc, had been an invalid for thirteen years before their marriage and unable to continue his profession. He had lived for the most part with his mother Madame Louise Belloc at her

4

house at La Celle. His premature death in 1872 was the result of a sunstroke. Louise Belloc was herself half Irish, daughter of a Colonel Swanton who took part in Napoleon's Russian campaign and had married a French wife. So that Belloc had Irish, as well as French and English blood in his veins.

Into these surroundings and influences the little Hilary (he was actually christened Hilaire after his grandfather, but was later known to his friends as Hilary) made his entry in the momentous year in which the Prussians entered Paris and the Pope withdrew into the precincts of the Vatican. Of the first eight years of his life, most of which were passed at the house at La Celle, his sister Mrs Belloc-Lowndes has given us a few details in her book *I, too, have lived in Arcadia*.

From that book we learn that at the age of four he wrote very much the same hand as in later life.

He learnt everything he was taught quickly and accurately, and when impressed by some dramatic and unexpected event he would compose a set of verses astonishing as to both thought and diction in a child of his age. . . . He early preferred verse to any other form of reading, and I find a letter written by my mother when he was five years old, saying that he was at that moment in a corner of the room, engaged in learning by heart, for his own pleasure, *The Lays of Ancient Rome*. He also took an intelligent and very eager interest in everything connected with scientific discoveries, in the past and the present.

In addition to these interests and talents we find that, while still a child, he was greatly attracted by the art and literature of Ancient Greece and Rome, took delight in geography and the making of maps, and even found to his taste descriptions of the English Parliament and its place in English life.

Just before the siege of Paris began—indeed travelling by the last train that left the capital—his parents with their two children moved to England and remained there until the siege was over, living for the greater part of the time in London. When they returned to France they found the house at La Celle almost in ruins and nearly all its contents pillaged or destroyed by the Germans. In spite of this, they decided to live on there and set about making the necessary repairs. It was not until 1878 that Madame Belloc let the house and went to live permanently in England. The reason for this was the loss of the greater part of her fortune. It became necessary for her to economize, and so, letting her house at La Celle, she took one in Slindon, at the foot of the Sussex Downs.

This was Belloc's first acquaintance with the county which was later to play so important a part in his life and his writings. For two years he passed the greater part of his time there with his mother in undisturbed enjoyment of the beauty of the surroundings. In 1880, however, he was sent as a boarder to the Oratory School at Edgbaston, which had recently been founded by Cardinal Newman. He remained there until 1887, but although he excelled in his school work and in the parts he took in the Latin plays performed annually by the boys, he never spoke with any enthusiasm of his school days. School discipline and the somewhat artificial life of a boarder at an English school no doubt grated upon one who had been accustomed to French ways and the unusual freedom his mother had allowed him.

In 1887 he left the Oratory with a sound background of classical education and brimming over with ideas which he was determined to express. Very early he was convinced that he could write and made up his mind to do so. His mother, however, was anxious that he should take up something less precarious than journalism or the writing of books. It seems that, in spite of her own literary activities and interest in education, she had little understanding of the talents of her own children. She had also been, since her financial losses, eager to see her son settled in some permanent employment which would bring him in a sufficient income. The decision she came to was to apprentice him to a local farmer on the Duke of Norfolk's estate, presumably with the intention that he should later take up farming on his own account. The success of such a project was from the start unlikely, for, though in later years, when he was well established as an author, he did take an interest in the farming of some 150 acres close to King's Land, his mind was far too full of literature and politics to be satisfied with life on the land as his main occupation. In addition to this he found the farmer to whom he was apprenticed uncongenial, so the experiment lasted only a short time, and he was soon trying his hand at journalism under the aegis of W. T. Stead, who was a friend of the family.

The following year he met Elodie Hogan and became engaged to her. The Hogans were an Irish family which, two generations before, had emigrated to California as the result of the famine in Ireland. Elodie and her sister Elizabeth were in 1889 on a visit to England and had had an introduction to Madame Belloc. It was not until 1896 that they were married, for there were several obstacles to be surmounted. In the first place Mrs Hogan, Elodie's mother, was not inclined to consent to her daughter's marriage to an impetuous young Frenchman with no present means of livelihood. Secondly, Elodie herself had half decided that she had a vocation for the religious life of a nun, and she actually entered a convent at Baltimore and remained there for a month. A third cause of the delay of their marriage was Belloc's liability, as a French citizen (for he was not naturalized as an Englishman till 1902), to serve his term in the French Army. Though he was now living in England and might, no doubt, have been able to escape this service, Elodie strongly advised him to present himself for it, so that he should never feel that he had avoided a duty owed to his native country. Then, finally, there was the question of earning a living.

His year as a Gunner with the 10th Battery of the 8th Regiment of Artillery (he was with the colours from November 1891 to August 1892) was passed at the frontier town of Toul and had a great influence upon his life. Not only did it give him a lasting love for the rough camaraderie of the French Army and a profound hatred of the Prussian, but it also developed the strong republicanism which was a feature of all the earlier part of his life, and increased in him his interest for topography and military history. It was there, too, that he learnt the numerous French marching songs which he continued to sing to the end of his life.

After his term of service it was arranged that he should go up to Oxford. He won an open scholarship to Balliol. His four years as an undergraduate left another deep impression upon his life, for right up to his death he would speak with affection of his old college and tell stories of what used to go on there, of Benjamin Jowitt who was Master when he first went up, and of the exploits of his many friends, to whom he remained attached all through life. His career at Oxford was a brilliant one. He won a high reputation as a speaker at the Union and eventually became its President. He carried off the Brackenbury Scholarship for history and obtained a brilliant first in his Schools. He confidently expected a college Fellowship, which Jowitt had virtually promised him, but when the time came for the election of new Fellows, a new Master had succeeded Jowitt, and his name did not appear on the list. This was a grievous disappointment to him (and one which rankled in his mind all through his life) especially as, in the expectation of a secure income, he had married Elodie and taken a house in Oxford. Actually it is extremely doubtful whether his vigorous temperament and the variety of his interests could have been satisfied by the limited outlets that life as a Don would have offered him. However that may be, his failure to obtain a Fellowship made it necessary for him to earn what money he could by writing books, giving University Extension lectures, coaching undergraduates, and re-entering the field of journalism. Although these means of obtaining a livelihood were both strenuous and precarious, they mapped out a course for which he was naturally suited. For he had always been determined to write and his political views had been developing through all the years since he was a child.

Necessity thus hastened the moment at which he entered the lists of authorship, and it is interesting to see what particularly occupied his mind at that time. Typically, the first book he published was a collection of verse, which he later withdrew from circulation, but retained some of the poems in subsequent collections. For the rest, his earliest books were concerned with the French Revolution (*Danton* and *Robespierre*) and with satires of the donnish mind (*Lambkins Remains*). In addition he produced the first four of his books of light verse that have enjoyed lasting popularity (*The Bad Child's Book of Beasts*, *More Beasts for Worse Children*, *The Modern Traveller*, and *A Moral Alphabet*). There also appears in these early years his book *Paris*, which showed what a profound knowledge he had of its history and topography at this early age.

From Oxford, in 1900, he moved to Chelsea and rented a house overlooking the river in Cheyne Walk. He remained there for some five years and would not have left had not the house been sold over his head. During this period the best known book that he published was *The Path to Rome*, the result as we shall see in a later chapter of a walk that he took in a straight line from Toul to Rome. *Avril*, a collection of essays on the poetry of the French Renaissance, was another important book written during these years. There also appeared the first of his satirical novels, *Emmanuel Burden*, with illustrations by Gilbert Chesterton, who had become his close friend and frequently visited him at his house in Chelsea.

On leaving Chelsea he returned to Sussex and lived for a year or so at Slindon until he could find in the county a house that he could buy and make his permanent home. In 1906 he discovered King's Land and moved there with his family of five children. King's Land was to be his home until his death in 1953, but although he always had a deep affection for it and, as we have seen, found time to interest himself in the land close by that he had bought to farm, his numerous activities continually called him away. He had for some years been writing and speaking in support of the Liberal Party and of Liberal Parliamentary candidates, and in 1906 he entered Parliament himself. In addition to this he was constantly travelling on the Continent, seeking topographical, and even seasonal, data for such books as *Marie Antoinette* and other studies of the French Revolution, the battles of Marlborough's campaigns, Napoleon's campaign against Russia in 1812, and many other of his historical writings. There were also numerous descriptive travel books, and essays which owed their origin to his journeyings. In England, too, his interest in history and topography kept him continually on the move. His books on *The Stane Street*, *The Old Road*, *The River of London*, *The Historic Thames*, *Warfare in England*, etc. all required detailed observation in different parts of the country. Nor was it only in Europe that he travelled. As a young man of nineteen he had crossed the Atlantic and made his way, mostly on foot, across the United States to California, exchanging pictures he had drawn *en route* for his board and lodging; and later in life he returned there over and over again, lecturing and visiting his American friends.

From 1906 to 1911 he had the additional work of a Member of Parliament, and this necessitated much time spent in London and visits to his constituency of South Salford, yet King's Land always remained the centre of his life. In 1911, dissatisfied with what he found in the House of Commons, he resigned and founded a weekly paper, *The Eye Witness*, in order to attack the evils he saw in the parliamentary system and to express his own political views.

A glance at the books he published round about this period shows the extraordinary variety and breadth of his interests. Although his disgust at the methods of party politics and parliamentary government, as he had experienced them from the inside, caused him to spend much of his time in writing books (such as *The Party System* and *The Servile State*) and articles to expose these evils, and although between 1911 and 1913 he was occupied in bringing to light to the best of his ability the particular corruptions of the Marconi scandal, yet he could find the time and the detachment to produce during those years three novels, three volumes of essays, an account of the French Revolution, a book of light verse, several detailed descriptions of famous battles, and *The Four Men*. Surely a feat of almost incredible energy and a signal testimony to the scope of a many-sided intelligence!

In 1914 there fell upon him the greatest sorrow of his life. His wife Elodie died at the early age of forty-two, and he never ceased to mourn for her. This is not the place, nor am I in any way competent to attempt a description of one whose saintliness, humour, and unceasing charity made her loved by everyone who met her. Her acute literary judgement was over and over again a great help to Belloc, and her unwavering faith strengthened his. Her death and the outbreak of war caused great changes in Belloc's life. Thenceforward he always wore black clothes, and for some years he wrote few books. After unsuccessfully presenting himself for service with the Army, he was persuaded by James Murray Allison, who had just broken his connexion with the Northcliffe Press and bought a weekly review called *Land and Water*, to write weekly articles on the progress of the war. These, combined with periodic visits to the front, filled much of his time, and, later on, became so widely read and so popular that he was in constant demand throughout the country for lectures on the strategy and tactics of the war. For the first time in his life he began to earn a considerable income, and in addition to King's Land he took a house in London. But he was not a man to accumulate money. He rarely invested it, and was recklessly generous. He loved the good things of life—travel, good food, good wine—and loved his friends to have them too. I have never known him refuse anyone a request for help if he could by any means comply with it. So, when the war was over and his articles and lectures on it came to an end, he was in much the same position financially as when it started.

From 1918 onwards he applied himself again with all the old energy to the writing of books, and perhaps more than ever his astonishing versatility becomes apparent. *The Contrast* shows a profound study of the differences between American and English ways of life; *The House of Commons and the Monarchy* marks a new development in his political thought; *The Jews* sums up his views (often misunderstood) on the problems that the diaspora of that energetic race has brought in its train. The first volume of his *History of England* and further researches into French history, a book on economics, two more volumes of essays, *The Cruise of the Nona*, another novel, that magnificent piece of satire *The Mercy of Allah*, and a number of books and pamphlets on religious subjects and on the war and military strategy—all these (and the list is not a complete one) made their appearance between 1918 and 1925.

In such a variety of output—which continued for as long as he went on writing—it is difficult to trace particular trends in his general out-look, but I think it may be said that the latter years of his writing life were devoted pre-eminently to historical studies and books specifically concerned with the Catholic Faith. These two subjects were linked closely together in his mind, indeed history was for him the reactions of mankind to the religion that created the civilization of Europe, and most of his books on the Catholic Faith were historical in character. But to the end he was, in addition, producing numerous books of travel, novels, light verse, and new poems.

Thus at my first meeting with him in 1921 he was at the height of his powers. Books were pouring from his pen, and his life was one of almost incredible activity. He had little or no money beyond what he was earning from his work, but he had many friends with whom he kept in constant contact, and to the end of his life he was adding new ones from the younger generation. Indeed he had an extraordinary gift for friendship and for inspiring it in others.

Such then was the background of the man who came first into my life in 1921, and who was, the next year, to become my father-in-law. From that time onwards until his death in 1953 I saw him frequently at irregular intervals, and during his last years, after a severe illness had left him incapable of further literary work, Eleanor kept house for him, and King's Land was our home.

2 Comings and Goings

MY engagement to Eleanor in 1922 came as something of a shock to Belloc. A Protestant and a school master—that was a combination of attributes he would certainly not have chosen for his future son-in-law. His summing up of the situation was characteristic. 'But, my darling child, that is almost as bad as marrying a parson.' Nor was the somewhat Victorian interview I had with him in the drawing-room at King's Land to discuss the matter altogether encouraging. We talked at some length about my financial position and the difficulties that might arise when a Catholic marries a non-Catholic. He seemed somewhat relieved when I told him that I owned a small house in Horsham and that I was far from feeling any aversion to the Catholic Faith, but his gloom did not entirely lift, and his parting words 'Well, I suppose we must go on with it' were hardly enthusiastic. But, as I came to realize when I got to know him better, and especially after I had been received into the Church, his stiffness of manner at this interview was the result of the profundity of his own faith and his anxiety lest anything should interfere with the faith of his daughter. Thereafter I never experienced from him anything but kindness, generosity, and friendly companionship.

So long as we had a non-Catholic school, before I became a Catholic, there were, it is true, some embarrassing moments, but the embarrassment, where it existed, was on our side only. Belloc had accepted the situation and was sublimely oblivious of the rather petty conventions of preparatory school life. He would every now and then offer to give a lecture to the boys, and would suggest that the Reformation or some equally controversial historical subject would interest them. I have no doubt it would have done so, for he was a born teacher and could hold the attention of any audience with the lucidity and directness of his exposition. But there were the non-Catholic parents to be considered, who might well have taken exception to Belloc as the interpreter to their sons of the religious upheaval of the sixteenth century. I would gently suggest some innocuous alternative subject, and he would—with a little disappointment perhaps—acquiesce and delight everybody with a vivid description of the Roman roads in England, or battles of the past, or even the elements of surveying.

He loved to keep in touch with all his friends and those he was fond of, and however busy he was, he always seemed to find time to hunt them up wherever they might be. So we not infrequently had visits from him, even when we had moved away from Horsham to Eridge and later to the Midlands. He would arrive in the wake of a series of telegrams, probably exhausted and hungry, usually, it seemed, in the middle of some school function. On one occasion school sports were going on and, after the prize-giving, my partner, who was retiring at the end of the term, was making a farewell speech to parents sitting on the cricket field in an attentive semi-circle facing him. I was on his left, due to pronounce a few platitudes suitable to the occasion as soon as he had finished. Belloc, with his thoughts far away, wandered up and took his place beside me. As my partner was reaching his peroration, I heard a high-pitched whisper on my left which must have carried half across the cricket ground. 'Rex, I wonder if you could think of a Latin tag that would give the sense of——' and here he mentioned some English saying that I have forgotten. It was typical of his utter unselfconsciousness. When uninterested in what was happening round him, his mind would be busy with thoughts of his own and he would suddenly come out with some remark or question quite unconnected with anything that was going on. I have heard him break into a trivial conversation with some wholly irrelevant remark such as 'What is fame, and why do men desire it?' and, thenceforward (such was the influence of his personality) interest would be aroused and the talk would be transformed into a discussion (sometimes largely a monologue) on the distinctions between fame and publicity and the strange hankering of human beings to be remembered for their achievements after their death.

At other times the impact of his surroundings upon his intensely critical mind would have more disconcerting consequences. I remember another visit he paid to us at our school. This time he arrived in the middle of a performance by the boys of a Gilbert and Sullivan opera.

Eleanor guided him to a seat in the crowded hall, and for some minutes he looked rather wearily at the stage where a small boy was singing a solo. Once again in that piercing stage whisper came the remark, 'That little boy is singing flat.' And then, shortly afterwards, bending over towards Eleanor: 'My darling, let's get out of this, I am exhausted.' Having extracted him with some difficulty from the congested lines of chairs, Eleanor piloted him through the dark with a torch up a steep pathway to the house. There, he expressed a desire for eggs and bacon and a bottle of wine. While these were being got ready for him (with some difficulty in the middle of preparing refreshments for the guests) he discoursed with interest on the rejection by Parliament of the new edition of the Prayer Book, having apparently quite forgotten the concert and gathering of parents, and, when he had eaten, cheerfully took his leave and started back to King's Land, some forty miles away, in his car.

These visits, however disorganizing they might temporarily be, were always prompted by a genuine desire to see those he loved, and he delighted to fit them into a day of innumerable engagements, often at the expense of much energy and long hours without food. It is only necessary to glance at almost any page of his diary to get an idea of his incredible activity. Here, for example, is one taken at random.

Thursday, 22nd January 1920. Got up just before 8 and went to 8 o'clock Mass. Elizabeth (his younger daughter) came down afterwards and went off by the 10 o'clock train. I dictated to Miss Phelan 5,000 words (Two MSS for *The New Statesman* and one for the *Illustrated London News*). Bought white port at Docman's on Squire's recommendation. Lunched with Foster at the Reform Club and met again the Member for Brighton, whose name I forget, but who has shaved off his beard. Went to the Road Club Board Meeting and thence to Mrs Asquith's, where we tried the cinema. I looked in at the Royalty Theatre, and then dined at the Beefsteak Club alone. Went back to the Royalty Theatre. I got home about 12 o'clock, walking, a fine night. Before going to bed saw Somerset at his window. He would not come out, as he was already going to bed.

That is no exceptional day for Belloc, but just common form during the active years of his life. No wonder that he used the moments between concentrated work and his many engagements in meditation, and that this meditation now and then divorced him from his surroundings. What is more surprising is that he could switch over so quickly and readily to song, gaiety, and light-hearted repartee with his friends. Most of them will, I think, remember him best in these joyous moods when all his immediate problems and worries would disappear in a flash and he would lift a whole roomful of people out of boredom or depression. It is hard to put one's finger on the qualities that made his conversation so attractive to so many different kinds of people. To Fleet Street I think it was the emphasis with which he used to express unusual views, combined with a fund of good stories and satirical digs at accepted institutions and personalities. These unusual views, never expressed for effect, though calculated to switch the minds of his listeners from the well-worn grooves of popular discussion which he so often despised, might relate to persons or events. Their first impact inspired surprise, perhaps half-amused incredulity (another Belloc *mot* to be stored in the memory and repeated later as a typical extravagance), but, when seriously considered, they had a way of appearing as shafts of light from a wider horizon of judgement than was familiar to the current opinions of the moment. Here is a single example of what I mean. When most people's minds were occupied with the cataclysm of war and its vast effects upon life in the world, Belloc would often repeat that the greatest event of this century was the regaining of political freedom by the Irish. It is true that he had a profound admiration and love of the Irish people and was never tired of emphasizing the key position they held in the various countries—especially the United States—to which they had emigrated, but his statement went much further than admiration. He saw in the long-awaited restitution of full liberty to Ireland a tremendous fulfilment of historical justice, and one that had been achieved by the nation itself against seemingly impossible odds. Viewed impartially from a point outside of the clamour of immediate preoccupations can it be said that his statement was untrue?

To those belonging to what he habitually called the Governing Class, amongst whom he had made many friends when at Balliol, it was the liveliness and vigour of his company together with his subtle under-standing of their way of life. He never tired of telling them that he belonged to a class different from theirs and of pointing out the short-comings of all the English social classes, including their own. But there is no doubt that he was happy in their friendship, and they in his. Another set of people with whom he got on famously was (paradoxi-cally to those who did not know him well) the Jews. I have seen him in a drawing-room, surrounded by Jews all eagerly talking to him and obviously enjoying his company and—more surprising still—he was discoursing to them on the Jewish problem and explaining his views on it. It is a complete mistake to suppose that he disliked Jews personally. What he felt about the race, as he has clearly set out in his book on the subject, was that its members should not conceal their nationality or pass themselves off as Englishmen, Frenchmen, Germans, etc. There is no doubt too, that he saw the dangers in political Jewry, but for indivi-dual Jews he had no antipathy and numbered several among his friends.

With children Belloc was usually popular. He fascinated them by doing surprising and delectable things, such as carrying them off at bedtime in their dressing-gowns to look at the moon through a big telescope, or making realistic birds out of paper that flapped their wings when you pulled their tails. In fact he broke all the nursery rules and talked to them with great seriousness in language that they could not understand, and, for that reason, greatly appreciated. I remember one small boy being brought to say goodbye to him. Belloc shook hands with him punctiliously and then remarked with the utmost solemnity 'Never forget, my boy, that you have today shaken hands with the great Rudyard Kipling.' The child seemed duly impressed, but later asked his mother, 'What is Rudyard Kipling?' Now and then his broad, black figure would inspire fear, but that was exceptional, and alarm would usually soon give place to interest, and interest to friend-ship. For though he could be a stern parent and a rebuker of familiarities, in his heart Belloc idealized children and wrote of them and to them with deep feeling. That he understood what would amuse them is borne out by the perennial popularity of the *Cautionary Tales*.

If conversation with his friends was a delight to him in which he

17

indulged on all possible occasions, work was a consuming fire into which he plunged for hours together with a concentrated zeal I have rarely, if ever, seen equalled. He emerged from these long bouts of concentration exhausted, but, such were his powers of recuperation and the strength of his will, that in an incredibly short time he would be singing songs or hurrying off to keep some appointment. All signs of fatigue would have vanished. But there were times, especially in the later years of his active life, in which the exhaustion would persist. He would sleep badly and show nervousness about his health. These moods, however, seldom lasted long, and any suggestion that he should consult a doctor was met with a tirade upon the dangers of submission to professional treatment. His own cure for most bodily ills was wine or an occasional glass of brandy and water, and on the whole this seemed to answer very well.

One day, it is true, I remember him returning to King's Land from London with a badly poisoned finger which he held up in front of him wrapped up in unwieldy bandages which he had procured from heaven knows where. With difficulty Eleanor persuaded him to see a doctor. A young assistant of his family doctor duly arrived and was at once warned by Belloc that he must do nothing that would cause physical pain. They retired together to a bathroom. The ordeal there for the young doctor, who was not used to dealing with patients of so determined a kind, must have been acute, for he came downstairs looking thoroughly shattered. Belloc on the other hand had recovered his good spirits, and triumphantly waving a newly bandaged finger called for drinks. They appeared to have exchanged the roles of doctor and patient.

But usually Belloc's teak-like constitution would carry him through the strains of overwork. Without this fundamental good health he would long ago have collapsed, for, once launched upon a train of thought, time vanished for him, and he pursued it to the end. Two attributes were principally responsible for this power of prolonged concentration. The number and variety of his strongly held views were a continual incitement to him to find expression for them, and his flair for probing to the heart of the matter about which he was seeking information was phenomenal. He seemed to know instinctively where to find references, sometimes of the sketchiest kind, to the subject in hand. These would lead him on swiftly to others more precise, until, like a hound on the trail, he came up with his quarry. The rapidity with which he extracted from one authority after another what he needed for his purpose demanded not only flair, but concentration of an unusual kind. It also explained to some extent the volume of his historical writings. In the end the strain of this immense output of energy became apparent. After his serious illness in 1941, following the collapse of France and the death of his son Peter, his powers of mental concentration left him, and he wrote no more.

It seems likely that the ability to fix his mind on a subject to the exclusion of what was happening around him was a big element in his fluency when lecturing or dictating an article. He told me once, when I had been trying to keep up in long hand with his flow of words as he dictated an article, that as a subject took form in his mind it fell almost automatically into paragraphs, and once he had begun to dictate he could see the structure of his sentences and rarely had to hark back and rearrange them. None the less, when he was writing a book he usually wrote down with his own hand a number of passages of special importance, which he would introduce in their places into his dictation. Nor was it only the structure of what he had to say that he mastered in dictating. The words he used and his style adapted themselves (without effort, it seemed) to his subject. One afternoon, after a bout of influenza, he came down in his dressing-gown still quite knocked out by his illness, and from an armchair asked me if I would take down one or two notes for the paper he was editing. We rushed through several of these at top speed, and then he said, if I could spare the time, he would like to write a short article. The words poured out with the same rapidity but in a style quite different from the staccato of the notes. This finished, I thought he must be exhausted and suggested a rest on the sofa. Instead, he told me that it was his habit to write at least 1,000 words of his history each day, and that day he had not done so, so, if I was not tired . . . And off he went again, his style once more entirely changing. It was a remarkable achievement for a sick man and would have been impossible unless his mind had been able to department and store up, not only a number of quite separate trains of thought, but the shape of the sentences and the style in which they were to be expressed.

With his verse it was otherwise. A single poem often took him years to complete and polish to his satisfaction. 'Tarantella', though so short, was two years in the making, and 'The Heroic Poem in Praise of Wine' still longer. Evidently the Muse, in which he believed, did not hand out her gifts ready made. Polyhymnia was less prompt in her response than Clio.

The filing of this tremendous output of prose and verse, together with the countless letters and telegrams that he received, was a stupendous undertaking, but one to which he attached considerable importance. Scarcely anything he received through the post or by telegram was destroyed. He handed over everything to his secretary to dispose of under a classification of which the initial letter of the writer or the subject of the particular document decided the file into which it was to go. Sometimes, when the accumulation of papers began to get beyond the powers of the secretary to deal with, he would invite everyone in the house to help in sorting out the pile. His organization of these sessions was almost military in its precision. We would be ranged round the dining-room table with sheets, each marked with a letter of the alphabet, covering its surface. The unwieldy mass of papers to be filed was brought in, and everybody set to work, as in a game of patience, piling them up one by one on the appropriate letter. Numerous difficulties would arise as to which pile a particular document should be assigned, arguments would break out and the wildest views be expressed, in fact the whole business ran the risk of becoming a glorious scramble, but an appeal to Belloc would at last decide the matter. This happened once over an invitation to meet the Queen of Rumania at a garden party at Buckingham Palace. The answer came at once: 'Q for Queens.'

It is difficult to explain this insistence of his on filing so many papers that were of no apparent use either to him or anybody else. I do not think that it had anything to do with a desire for fame in future years, for the only thing that he ever expressed a wish to be remembered by was his verse, and he had a violent abhorrence for all kinds of cheap publicity, indeed he did everything possible to avoid anything of the sort and, as can be seen from his writings, ridiculed those who sought it. For this reason, I think, he refused to publish an autobiography, though he was often pressed to do so. The explanation more probably lies in his strong feeling for tradition—a feeling which at times was not unmixed with superstition. Whatever came into the house (his home, which in so many respects was steeped in tradition) was itself, in his eyes, an addition, however small, to that tradition. To destroy the accumulation of the years was something of a sacrilege. For tradition and what most people would call superstition played a large part in his life. He had, for example, a great esteem, almost a reverence, for lineage, that framework of family tradition, looking upon it as a valuable element in the continuity of history and therefore a thing to be proud of whatever the rank and station of the family in question. To walk through the rooms of King's Land was to make a journey into the past. The pictures, the statues, the furniture, the books, even the hundred and one things he had picked up on his travels or been given by friends or his children, were treasured landmarks in his life and the lives of his forebears. For years a toy stork, suspended on a wire from the ceiling, which had been given to him by his daughter, used to swing to and fro as the door of the room opened. This became a tradition and stories collected round it. Almost traditional too (so long did it fulfil its humble task) was a visiting card that had been thrust between two live wires of an electric bell at a point where the insulation was worn. Yellow with age, it still remained in position years after it had been put there as a temporary expedient.

The superstitious side of Belloc's nature is more difficult to account for. Yet it certainly existed. In some instances it was little more than a respect felt for practices that had grown up in the course of years, discontinuance of which appeared in the light of a severance with tradition and therefore apt to bring bad luck. But there were other actions which he seemed to view with abhorrence for no evident reason, such as bringing into the house may blossom, broom, or pea-cocks' feathers. No doubt these may be country superstitions which he had met with in his youth and adopted, but they sat strangely upon one of such robust reasoning power and such directness in his dealings with life. Perhaps to some extent an explanation of this side of him may

21

be found in his acute awareness of the participation of the spiritual in everyday actions and events. He had a profound regard for the souls of those who had been dear to him in life and was constant in his observance of certain anniversaries. But this was a part of his make-up of which most of his acquaintances knew nothing, so vigorous were his reactions to current events and to material things. He was neither introspective, save occasionally when suffering physically, nor did he, as a rule, realize what was going on in other people's minds, although he has made so many penetrating studies of the minds of historical characters. He frequently seemed to be uncertain of his age and would have overlooked his own birthdays had he not been reminded of them by others.

In the latter part of his life these reminders came to him from his large circle of friends and admirers. The dinner that they gave him on his sixtieth birthday was a joyous affair. Writers and journalists predominated, but there were many friends from all walks of life. Mgr Ronald Knox, who could not be at the dinner, sent a charming tribute in Latin Sapphics, which was printed on cards and handed round to all present. There were to be no speeches, except an explanatory word from A. D. Peters, Belloc's literary agent and close friend, who had been mainly responsible for arranging the meeting. However, this rule was not so much broken as completely reversed. Instead of there being no speeches, *everybody* made a speech. The joke started, innocently enough, by Peters associating 'The gentleman on my left' with arrangements for the dinner. The latter at once got to his feet and, after a few words, passed responsibility to 'the gentleman on *his* left'. This started the ball rolling, and it did not stop until it had rolled round all the tables. A. P. Herbert and Duff Cooper provided particularly brilliant extemporizations, the former addressing an imaginary meeting of 'old comrades' and the latter giving a lifelike imitation of Lloyd George making an impassioned speech in the House of Commons. Maurice Baring contributed, with the utmost solemnity, a schoolboy rendering of one of Mgr Knox's stanzas. And so it went on, a light-hearted, but very genuine, tribute to the guest of the evening.

The seventieth birthday celebration—a lunch at the Dorchester— was not so happy. It had to be put off until 1941, and the anxieties of war overshadowed it. Nor was Belloc himself well. The collapse of France had shaken him badly, and in the few formal speeches made there was none of the spontaneity and gaiety of 1930.

The party at King's Land, however, in July 1950 made up for the rather gloomy war-time anniversary. It was a perfect sunny afternoon and more than 400 guests were there to show their affection and admiration for their host. Belloc, though infirm, had made a wonderful recovery from his illness and was in high spirits. He sat amongst his friends and entertained all with talk, talk that still reflected most of the Bellocian moods, in its jesting and its unexpectedness. Once, as I passed by the group round him he asked, 'Would one of you do something for me?' There was immediately a movement of readiness to help. He continued at once: 'I should like somebody to bring me a large bag full of gold.' Nor did the full day appear to tire him. Ten or twelve friends came in for lunch, and about the same number, mostly members of the family, to supper in the evening, when almost all his songs, with the tunes he had made for them, were sung, and many others besides, in all of which he took part.

I think many will recall the happiness of that day when they think of Belloc and regret the loss of so vivid and virile a personality.

3 *Belloc's Creative Genius*

BELLOC used often to say that the writer's trade was a vile one. This may seem an ungracious remark when made by one who had received a full measure of praise for his books and had obviously enjoyed writing at least some of them. Yet it was not the mere complaint of a disillusioned professional man against the profession he had followed. It was much more genuine than that. Writing, for Belloc (except verse, which he put into a different category), was little more than a vehicle for the expression of his views, for pillorying what he held to be false, and for influencing the thought and action of his fellow men. The fluent oratory of his public speaking had the same purpose. But what he set store by was the views themselves. The vehicle might break down or prove ineffective, but the views persisted and were of paramount importance. There might be other ways of getting them accepted. Thomas Derrick once described to me an incident which he had witnessed, typical of the younger Belloc. He was addressing a generally hostile audience on the subject of private, as against State, ownership. One heckler had been particularly persistent in his interruptions. Belloc broke off and addressed him: 'I should prefer, sir, to settle this question by physical encounter, but since the rules of this club do not permit that method, I am compelled to attempt the task of teaching you how to think.' Words had failed. He would have liked to try another way. That incident, though cast in an exaggerated form, does, I think, show his opinion of the inadequacy of words.

He has been constantly praised as a master of prose and we have seen how he could change his style to suit his subject. Moreover, his interest in language was intense—the derivations and histories of words and the subtle art of turning the words and thoughts of one language into those of another intrigued him. His essay on Translation is a valuable contribution to the practice of this art. He knew that the vehicle that served him was a delicate one and required careful supervision, but his greatest gift did not lie in that. It was the substance of what he had to say—the creative genius of his mind—that marked him out as an outstanding personality. Had he never written a book or delivered a public speech, he would have impressed himself upon his fellows by this power of creation.

Imaginative creation is in some degree common to all writers, as it is to all artists. When one speaks of a man doing creative work, one thinks of painters interpreting their thoughts on canvas, of novelists inventing characters and situations, of historians forging links between the events they chronicle, of philosophers approaching truth from new angles, and so on. But Belloc possessed more than fertility of imagination or the ability to impress his individuality upon a subject. He introduced into the world's stock of knowledge new ideas and new ways of interpreting facts already known. He had, it seemed, an intuitive grasp of essentials and a point of view that was almost wholly independent of the conclusions arrived at by others. These characteristics were evident in everything he did as well as in his writings. When, for example, he visited a town, or a building, or a locality hitherto unknown to him, he would approach it from an angle of his own choosing, deserting the well-trodden ways of sight-seers. This was far from being a conceit or a desire to appear original (he had absolutely no conceit in his make-up), but from an intuitive perception of what he was about to see and how that could be done to the greatest advantage. In his writing everywhere there is this same freshness of approach to his subject, and it is particularly noticeable because his written words approximate so closely to his conversation and the form of his thought. There is no artificial veneer imposed upon them and no striving for effect. Examples abound in all his work. The quality of his satire in the Chester-Belloc novels, and most of all perhaps in that little masterpiece *The Mercy of Allah*, has a distinctive personal note entirely his own; his numerous essays, characterized by his masterly use of digression as a main ingredient, might be the man himself talking and laughing with his friends; his rhetorical passages have an unadorned force wholly consistent with the strength and directness of conviction; even his comic verse, so peculiarly Bellocian, is a creation distinct from anything else in literature.

But there are particular books and surveys of events and tendencies that exemplify *par excellence* this creative side of his genius. His historical work has given a new contour to English history; his social studies have created a new formula for the establishment of widely diffused private ownership in the place of capitalism; and some of his books—notably *The Path to Rome* and *Belinda*—have introduced new genres into literature.

Let us look at these examples of his creative genius more closely, not so much with the object of proving the truth of his historical and social theses (they have already had a profound effect upon his generation), or the excellence of the other books I have mentioned, but rather in order to show the creative force of the mind that produced them.

As an historian Belloc used methods that differed from those of most writers of history. While lacking the immense specialized erudition of men like Coulton and Pollard, he based his conclusions on a survey of more varied evidence than they did, on the terrain where events took place, on monuments, pictures, and forms of building in various ages, on legend as a pointer to underlying truths, but most of all upon common sense and judgement of character. He approached a period of history and the men that influenced it in much the same way as he approached an unknown town or piece of country—with an eye untrammelled by perusal of guide books and with a flair for the discovery of essentials.

That of course is not to say that he omitted study of the written sources of history, but he submitted them to the same searching enquiry as he would a friend's recommendation of the food at such-and-such a restaurant. He was very much alive to the fact that distortions of the truth through advocacy of some cause were not confined to the present time.

This raises the question whether he was himself an advocate in his interpretation of history. The charge has often been brought against him. Did he, for instance, as a convinced Catholic, twist his history to suit his beliefs? To answer that question fully would require more space than I can afford here, but, speaking generally, the answer surely must be that all history is to a large extent a matter of individual interpretation. If facts speak for themselves, it is astonishing how many

26

different things they say. Belloc undoubtedly reacted strongly against the Whig history that had its origin in the eighteenth century, and desired to show up the falsity of many of its conclusions. Moreover he was firmly convinced that the Catholic Church had an immense influence on the course of events, but he was by no means an uncritical supporter of all the actions of its ministers. He looked upon it as a divinely appointed institution on which, together with ancient Greece and Rome, the civilization of Europe was founded, and it was thus for him the touchstone—in spite of the admitted errors of individual Catholics—against which that civilization should be tested. The fact that he frequently quoted with approval Newman's dictum that all wars are religious wars shows that the distinction he drew between the aims of different people was one of religion rather than of race or class. If that is advocacy, then all historians must be counted as advocates, for no man can write history without introducing opinions that he has formed from a study of events.

But for our purpose here the question is not so much what influenced Belloc's mind—as all minds must in one way or another be influenced—in forming his opinion of the significance of historical events, but rather in what ways he shed a new light upon them.

I have said that he has given a new contour to English history. The first lines of this contour appear in his emphasis upon the Roman rather than the Anglo-Saxon origins of the English people. Following upon that is his insistence upon the close relationship that existed between England and the Continent—especially France—in the years prior to the advent of William the Conqueror, and the European outlook that the Crusades exemplified in later years. What he has called 'The High Middle Ages'—that is, the thirteenth and early fourteenth centuries—owed its importance to the continuation of this welding of England into European civilization based upon the Catholic Faith. Magna Carta, which many historians count as a turning point in history, is for him no more than a confirmation of existing customs, effected by a 'rebellion of the rich' against the onerous taxation that King John's efforts to hold his possessions in France had necessitated.

The decline of the Middle Ages, according to Belloc, was largely brought about by the Black Death in the middle of the fourteenth century, which he calls somewhere the watershed of English history. He enumerates a number of results of this plague which decimated the population of England. Amongst these were a change of language from the French of the upper classes and the Anglo-Saxon dialects of poorer people to the English of Chaucer and *Piers Plowman*. This he considered cut England off to some extent from the general culture of the Western Continent. Other results of the Black Death were the gradual break up of the manorial system; a hardening of the Church's organization, due to the death of so many of the clergy and their consequent loss of touch with the laity, and the fall in the standard of religious training; and lastly, the growth of a revolutionary feeling among the people. All this, in his opinion, prepared the ground for the Reformation.

The Reformation itself, which for Catholics was the great disaster of English history, Belloc treats, so far as England was concerned, almost as an accident—the unfortunate infatuation of Henry VIII for Ann Boleyn—and though he points out contributory causes, some of which reflect upon the organization of the Church, he reserves his big guns of criticism for Henry's weakness in permitting the rise of a class of wealthy landowners—who were later to control and then destroy the monarchy—by distributing among them the large estates that had come into his hands from the dissolution of the Monasteries. His emphasis upon this change in the balance of power within the kingdom is especially marked in his interpretation of the reign of Queen Elizabeth. She appears as a thwarted woman almost wholly controlled by Burleigh—passionate yet physically deformed, vicious yet secretly hankering after the faith she had lost, and above all powerless. Her reign sounds the knell of English monarchy. It was the prelude of the Civil Wars and the execution of Charles I, and though there was a 'last rally' after the Restoration, from 1688 onwards the squires, and later the bankers, were in the saddle.

Belloc's treatment of Oliver Cromwell is equally individual. He disposes of the idea that the leaders of the Parliamentary revolution were spokesmen—still less members—of the poorer classes. They were for the most part squires or City merchants intent upon furthering their own interests, all part of the anti-monarchical clique raised up by Henry VIII's action in dissolving the monasteries.

Concurrently with the undermining of the monarchy come the beginnings of the destruction of the English peasantry. Belloc lays great stress upon this, pointing to the law known as the Statute of Frauds as the main instrument by which the peasant owner lost the title to his land and perforce became a landless labourer, foreshadowing the similar plight of the craftsman when the invention of machines was used as a pretext for industrializing the island and introducing capitalism.

As an ardent European, and holding, as he did, that England must be an integral part of Europe if her civilization was to survive, he was a strong supporter of Napoleon's attempt to unify the Continent. He was fully aware, however, as his book *Europe and the Faith* makes clear, that such unification could ultimately repose on nothing less solid than a common religious faith. His admiration for the thirteenth century was due to that unity, which underlay all the wars and political disputes of the period. He certainly was not one of those who looked upon it romantically as a golden age of material comfort.

His views upon the last two and a half centuries of English history (a period of which he has not written with the same fullness as of the earlier years) are those of a man who sees the expected results of past ill doing. The eighteenth century in England is marked chiefly by the rise of the money power, which he detested as the foe of liberty, and the reduction of the Catholic Church, which he held to be the bulwark of our civilization, to a despised refuge of a tiny, persecuted minority. In the nineteenth he saw the final extinction of the peasantry and the baneful results of the power wielded by industrial capitalism. For, to him, the 'prosperity' of the Victorian era was not only founded upon injustice, but unstable in itself. He was not one of those who considered that the riches of a class or cheap imported food constituted national prosperity.

Besides his more formal history, contained in four volumes which cover the years from the Roman occupation of Britain to the death of Robert Cecil in 1612, and a number of detailed studies of important historical characters, Belloc has introduced into many of his other books and essays sidelights upon the past, and has given illuminating reconstructions of historical events in his fascinating little volume entitled *The Eye Witness*. Indeed the historical bent of his mind was continually making itself evident in his talk whenever one accompanied him on a journey. His stored knowledge, obtained in so many diverse ways, seemed ever at hand wherever he travelled.

But the point that I am here trying to make is that this outline of the past, which he presents to us with such clarity and common sense, breaks new ground in its explanation of events and personalities. It marks a creative intelligence of an unusual kind. In some instances, it is true, other historians have followed much the same course as Belloc, as, for example, in recognizing the part that Ancient Rome plays in our origins and make-up, or in insistence upon the far-reaching effects of the Black Death, or in recording the disappearance of peasant ownership. In others his interpretation is unique—at all events in the priority of importance he gives to particular political and social factors, and to little-noticed traits in the characters of famous men. I have mentioned his contention that Burleigh and not Elizabeth was the effective monarch in England during the latter's reign. It was Burleigh, according to Belloc, through his intelligence and singleness of purpose, who became the leader and master mind among the clique of newly enriched landowners, and it was thus he who engineered the gradual elimination of the Catholic Faith in order to secure for their new owners the lands of the monasteries that had been dissolved. This vested interest of the squires in the land they had acquired further demanded that the power of the sovereign should be weakened and eventually transferred to themselves. This process, so successfully started by Burleigh, continued in Parliament's opposition to Charles I, in the Civil War, and finally in the removal and execution of the king.

Belloc's portrait of Oliver Cromwell also breaks new ground. He presents him as a man brought up in wealthy surroundings and nursing a bitter hatred for the Catholic Church, whose two principal attributes were mastery in intrigue and outstanding ability in tactical command of cavalry. He explodes the conflicting myths that in turn represented him as an unmitigated villain and a national hero.

But what makes Belloc's history distinctive is not merely his fresh approach to particular events and the men responsible for bringing them about, but especially his grasp of a logical sequence of cause and effect running through the centuries, a sequence illuminated by his understanding of human motives and the exercise of common sense. His work thus possesses a unity that is absent from so much historical writing. Specialized research tends to departmentalize periods and lose the synthesis of the whole story. Belloc sees history as a continuous panorama of the achievements, the intrigues, and the follies of mankind, each with its consequences for good and ill, strength and weakness. But the most important unifying principle of his work derives from his insistence upon the dominating effect of religious belief on men's actions. It is therefore likely to be challenged as misleading by those whose beliefs are opposed to his, or who set little or no store by religion in any form. Moreover, any interpretation of history that runs counter to what is familiar and generally accepted is not unnaturally suspect and will be submitted to a microscopic examination. Such a challenge has been frequently made and minor inaccuracies—from which his work is by no means free—and his reluctance to disclose the sources of his information are held up as evidence of the falsity of his general theses. On the other hand much of the new picture he paints is being tacitly accepted even by those whose views differ widely from his, and a crop of younger students of history has appeared which is following the trail he has blazed.

The social-economic conditions that Belloc advocated in such books as *The Restoration of Property*, *The Servile State*, *Economics for Helen*, and a multitude of pamphlets and articles were not in themselves a new creation, indeed he was at pains to point out that they are a norm best suited to the nature of man. His creative powers were here exemplified, partly in his ability to extricate himself from a social environment taken for granted by most Englishmen of his time, but chiefly in the arguments he used to support his theses and the plans he evolved whereby it might be possible to bring about the revolution he desired.

His work in this respect is at once an inspiration and a blueprint for those who continued it. His two friends Gilbert Chesterton and Father Vincent McNabb, both of whom came to see the truth of his contentions, did much—each in his own way—to explain and popularize them. But it was Belloc who first outlined the plan, and forced it upon the notice of an incredulous audience.

I have outlined in Chapter 4 the nature of this plan to re-introduce the ownership of widely distributed property among the people of England. He fully realized the immense difficulty of the task. 'I do not know,' he writes in *The Restoration of Property*, 'whether it be possible to start even the beginnings of a change. I doubt heavily that it is possible to plant successfully even the small seedlings of economic freedom in our society, here, in England, today.' But he continues: 'What I certainly know is that, failing such a change, our industrial society must necessarily end in the restoration of slavery. The choice lies between property on the one hand and slavery, public or private, on the other. There is no third issue.'

Starting thus with an almost universal opposition to, often ridicule of, his thesis, he proceeds first to array the arguments brought against it and to answer them by reference to the nature of human beings. This part of his work is in itself an essay in creative thought. He does not force his ideas upon his readers, but quite impartially and with the utmost clarity sets forth the arguments of the two sides—the capitalist and Communist on the one hand, his own on the other—and he admits that 'unless a sufficient number of our fellow-citizens feel with a sufficient degree of intensity that economic freedom is a good, economic freedom (that is, well-divided Property) can never be restored'.

He then proceeds to the task, never, I think, attempted before, of evolving ways of undermining the capitalist system (and at the same time and by the same means the socialist ideal of State ownership) and introducing in their place a society characterized by small and medium-sized ownership.

It is impossible in the space available to me here even to enumerate, still less to discuss, all the methods by which he would attempt to effect the change. Some of them have ceased to be practicable owing to the growth of centralized control since the time when his books were written. For we must remember that his plan of action was designed for the special conditions existing in England at the time of writing. Nor must we think (as Belloc over and over again warns us against thinking) that the proposals he makes would, if carried out, effect an immediate revolution of society. His aim is a strictly limited one: to encourage and safeguard small ownership where it still exists; to prevent the creation or continuance of large economic units where the nature of the instrument used does not necessitate large-scale working; and so, gradually to establish sporadic islands of economic freedom which might encourage the spread of independence elsewhere. But perhaps one example of his methods may help to show the creative nature of his work.

Dealing with the question of small, privately owned shops he proposes two converse economic policies: first, to handicap the large distributor by a system of differential taxation, steeply rising as the property increased in size, against chain shops, multiple stores, and retail turnover. This he would do in the case of multiple stores by the State-licensing of all the important categories of retail distribution, and by exacting a steeply rising tax as the number of categories in a single shop increased. In the case of chain shops and retail turnover a similar tax would become prohibitive after a certain number of shops or a certain figure in turnover had been reached.

The converse part of his policy he describes as follows:

> The money raised by the differential tax on large distribution . . . should be used to protect artificially the small man against the great. It should be used to establish and conserve corporate credit within the guild to which . . . the small distributor should belong; it should even be used, perhaps exceptionally, to subsidize the starting of the small man.

That is a single instance of the many original suggestions Belloc has put forward in pursuance of a policy of which many people approve, but which no one before him had seen a possible way of implementing. Nor is it only that each of these suggestions has been creatively conceived and the strength of the opposition to them assessed, but there is an order in the proposed action running through the whole plan— from the saving of the small distributor to the much more difficult tasks of curbing high taxation and breaking the monopoly of wholesale distribution—by which the first minor successes are made to lead on to and serve the major revolution of our economy.

Has all this constructive thought been wasted? I do not think so. A man cannot command success, and in this field Belloc was always highly doubtful of the possibility of success. Most people still talk of his ideas (often without reading his defence of them) as pipe dreams and uneconomic absurdities. Yet in the last decade or so each one of the political Parties has had recourse to them: 'a Property-owning Democracy', 'Co-ownership', and a tendency to return to an interpretation of socialism in the terms of Robert Owen rather than of Marx. That is not much perhaps. It is certainly still a long way from Belloc's incisive proposals, but it shows a slight movement in the direction he pointed out. It is noteworthy that there was a considerable demand for *The Servile State* before the last General Election.

As well as his history and his essays in social economics, Belloc has written one or two books which appear to me to create a new genre in literature. Of these I would note especially *The Path to Rome* and *Belinda*.

Of *Belinda* I will say no more here than that any sympathetic reader will find in it much more than a satire of upper-class conventions of the early nineteenth century. It is certainly that, but there is at the same time a compassionate—almost a nostalgic—feeling for the two young lovers and their fight against fate. Through the satire—so admirably clothed in the language of the more romantic nineteenth-century novelists—a very genuine beauty keeps appearing. And I think it must be these two contrasted themes, so perfectly fused, that makes *Belinda* one of the books that Belloc really enjoyed writing. For on more than one occasion he looked in at our house in Horsham bringing with him sheets of the *Belinda* manuscript that he had just completed and read them out to us with obvious relish. That was an unusual thing for him to do. I cannot recall any other occasion when I heard him read aloud from his manuscripts, though he often quoted his own verse from memory. I think he realized that in *Belinda* he had achieved something he had set out to do.

The Path to Rome is perhaps the most remarkable book that Belloc wrote. On the fly-leaf of a copy of it, in which he has made some notes and corrections, he has scribbled the envoi of a ballade of which the refrain runs: 'Alas! I never shall so write again!' If this refers, as it probably does, to the book in which it was written, it is in a sense true: nothing quite like *The Path to Rome* came from Belloc's pen again. That is not to affirm that it is the best book he ever wrote (though there are many people who think it is), but rather to suggest, what I am here trying to show, that it is a book without peers—a creation in literature.

What makes it so? Before trying to answer that question, let us look with complete detachment at the various ingredients that go to make up the matter of his book. The diary of a pilgrimage on foot in a straight line from Toul to Rome—frequent dissertations on the Catholic Faith, and constant references to its effect upon himself and others—long digressions full of his thoughts, his fears, his resolves— one vivid and heartbreaking account of his failure to cross the Gries Pass in a snowstorm—for the rest, walking, eating, sleeping, and high spirits mingling with exhaustion and depression. Not, one would have said, very promising material to submit to an English publisher at the turn of the century. Nor was it. More than twenty firms refused it, yet it has become a classic; in edition after edition its sales have continued; and it has been held up by competent judges of literature as a book to be read, not once only, but several times each year. What is the explanation?

I think that it is the outcome of a crisis in Belloc's life. It is a profession of faith. Belloc was of course a born Catholic. He was also born with a highly critical mind. It is probable that during his youth and early manhood, though he continued to practise his Faith, his general outlook was more affected by politics, history, and human companionship than by religion. The profound faith of his wife, however, soon brought him to a re-examination of the religion that in his heart he had never ceased to acknowledge. A letter which he wrote to his mother soon after his marriage seems to bear this out. In it he writes:

> We have been married in as Catholic a way as could be, with a nuptial Mass and Communion and all sorts of rites and benedictions, by an old Catholic Priest called Slattery. . . . She [Elodie] made me go to confession twice before risking the Sacrament, and I will believe what she believes and hold to what she and you hold to.

The rest of the evidence for the genesis of *The Path to Rome*, and the more immediate cause of its being written are to be found in the book itself. In his introduction—that glorious bravura 'In praise of this

35

Book'—he tells us how, when passing through the valley where he was born, he noticed that the church had been restored and went in.

> Moreover, saying my prayers there, I noticed behind the high altar a statue of Our Lady, so extraordinary and so different from all I had ever seen before, so much the spirit of my valley, that I was quite taken out of myself and vowed a vow there to go to Rome on Pilgrimage and see all Europe which the Christian Faith has saved; and I said, 'I will walk all the way and take advantage of no wheeled thing, I will sleep rough and cover thirty miles a day, and I will hear mass every morning; and I will be present at high mass in St Peter's on the Feast of St Peter and St Paul.'

That was the mood in which his pilgrimage was undertaken and completed.

But right in the middle of it, there was a new revelation—a revelation that was not only a blinding light upon what he had experienced at La Celle St Cloud (though it was indeed that), but at the same time a scorching flame that seemed to be burning up so many things that he had found delectable in life. It was at Undervelier, where, as he rested smoking a cigar by the stream, 'a bell began tolling, and it seemed as if the whole village were pouring into the church'. He followed and heard Vespers sung. He came out with (as he puts it)

> my whole mind taken up and transfigured by this collective act, and I saw for a moment the Catholic Church quite plain, and I remembered Europe and the centuries. Then there left me altogether that attitude of difficulty and combat which, for us others, is always associated with the Faith.

And then for three pages he considers the nature of belief. How, when youth is full on us, we reject it, 'like men who follow down the cleft of a mountain and the peaks are hidden from us and forgotten. It takes years to reach the dry plain, and we look back and see our home.' What are the reasons for our return? What are the hard things that we must undergo in exchange for this gift? He examines them all and ends upon a note of sadness which the casual reader might easily misinterpret: 'It is a good thing to have loved one woman from a child, and it is a good thing not to have to return to the Faith.'

The whole passage is a remarkable profession—perhaps one should say, renewal—of faith. It lays bare the whole purpose of the pilgrimage, and gives a new meaning to the book. If the sadness slips into the background, its note is never quite absent. But Belloc is still in the full vigour of his youth, and the revelation that came to him at Undervelier is far from diminishing it. Rather, it seems, he found in that youthful energy and gaiety an instrument for completing the task he had set himself and for infecting others with the revelation he had received. That, I am convinced, is the explanation why *The Path to Rome* is unique. It was inspired by an overpowering experience and written with every faculty sharpened by a tremendous discovery.

Such a revelation breaking upon a mind of the calibre of Belloc's was bound to produce a masterpiece. *The Path to Rome* is a book overflowing with supreme confidence, a confidence not of the writer in his own powers or of the pilgrim in his own endurance (he underlines his inability to express in words the vision within him or the non-fulfilment of vows that he had made), but in the illumination he had received; in the strong faith that reduced to comparative insignificance the satisfaction of intellect or the senses.

And yet there is a final passage in which earthly beauty is fused into this vision of the supernatural, setting a seal alike upon the purpose and the environment of the pilgrimage. It was at Sillano—a mere sixty miles from Rome :

> There alone I sat and watched the night coming up in these Tuscan hills. The first moon since the waning in Lorraine—(how many nights ago, how many marches!)—hung in the sky, a full crescent, growing into brightness and glory as she assumed her reign. The one star of the west called out his silent companions in their order; the mountains merged into a fainter confusion; heaven and the infinite air became the natural seat of any spirit that watched this spell. The fire-flies darted in the depths of vineyards and of trees below; then the noise of the grasshoppers brought back suddenly the gardens of home; and whatever benediction surrounds our childhood . . .

In very early youth the soul can still remember its immortal habitation, and clouds and the edges of hills are of another kind from ours, and every scent and colour has a savour of Paradise. What that quality may be no language can tell, nor have men made any words, no, nor any music to recall it—only in a transient way and elusive the recollection of what youth was, and purity, flashes on us in phrases of the poets, and is gone before we can fix it in our minds— oh! my friends, if we could but recall it! Whatever those sounds may be that are beyond our sounds, and whatever are those keen lives which remain alive there under memory—whatever is Youth —Youth came up that valley, at evening, borne upon a southern air. If we deserve or attain beatitude, such things shall at last be our settled state, and their now sudden influence upon the soul in short ecstasies is the proof that they stand outside time and are not subject to decay.

This, then, was the blessing of Sillano, and here was perhaps the highest moment of those seven hundred miles—or more.

If more is needed to prove the transcendental urge that gave birth to the book and made of it a creation apart from others, there is yet another sentence written on the fly-leaf of the copy I have already mentioned. It is dated 1904, two years after publication, when Belloc must have wished to emphasize once again the significance of his message. It runs : ' I wrote this book for the glory of God.'

4 *Rebel Reformer* ✶

A̲ᴌ̲ᴌ̲ through his life—though more noticeably in his younger days—Belloc was radical in the reforms he proposed. Failure to realize this important side of him leaves a great part of his life unexplained, and it is all the more necessary to emphasize it because, of late years and perhaps especially since his death, there has been a tendency to pass over—or at least to tone down—the strength of his opposition to many generally accepted habits and opinions of his fellow countrymen.

There are four main tests of the genuineness of a reformer: first, that his accusations are true; secondly, that he acts from a sense of justice and not of self-interest ; thirdly, that he is prepared to take personal risks in the course he is following, and fourthly, that he has a constructive remedy for the evils he is attacking. Although it may not always be possible to convince a critic that all these tests have been surmounted, I think that it will be generally agreed from a study of the revolutionary side of Belloc's life that he failed in none of them.

It is hard to pick out with exactness the early influences and experiences on a man's life that may later have had their effect upon his views and his actions. Moreover, besides environment and outside influences there is the inborn character of the individual man which shapes his attitude to life. In considering Belloc's revolt against so many of the social and political trends of his time one is tempted to explain his actions chiefly as the result of this inborn urge; for, as we have seen elsewhere, his creative genius seems to be singularly unconnected with

---

✶ The word 'rebel' strictly means one who resists duly constituted or lawful authority. I use it in this chapter, as applied to Belloc, in a somewhat looser sense of one who challenges the powers that be, with no implication that those powers had a lawful right to exercise authority in the points attacked. Belloc assailed practices and forms of government which he held to be corrupt or harmful. He never challenged authority as such.

the achievements of other men or the views expressed by them. So far as heredity goes, he was descended on the English and Irish sides of his family from men and women inspired by a strong sense of justice— Priestley who was driven from his country through refusal to compromise with principle; Joseph Parkes, whose unremitting work for the Reform Bill was prompted by a keen sense of justice; his Irish antecedents, the Swantons, who took up whole-heartedly the cause of Irish independence; and his own mother, who, though her strong feminist ideals were far from appealing to her son, yet displayed both courage and energy in her pursuit of them. Such a family history would lead one to expect in a descendant both independence and strength of character.

But there were, as well, experiences in Belloc's youth that confirmed and accentuated these natural traits. Prominent among these was his study of the French Revolution. That historic upheaval afforded substance for some of his earliest books, and undoubtedly made a deep impression on his mind. That is not to say that he was an uncritical admirer of all the principles that inspired it, still less of the methods it employed. But the republican ideal was strong in him from his earliest years, and his term of service in the French Army, which still felt itself to be the product of the revolutionary victors of Valmy, added to his democratic zeal. He had grown up, too, with people of republican views, and as soon as he had left school was eager to give practical expression to the convictions he held on justice and good government. During his years at Oxford he was a formidable speaker in the Union debates, and, when he had come down, he joined actively, as we have seen, in support of the Liberal Party, whose ideas he felt to be nearest to his own.

Here then were all the ingredients of revolt, but revolt, as he then imagined, as one of a Party devoted to the curbing of privilege and the consolidation of popular government. For it is important to remember that in those early days he had confidence in the House of Commons as a vehicle for effecting reforms. It was his experience inside it that changed him from being one of a group of reformers to a rebel fighting almost alone against the whole system and practice of Parliament as he saw it functioning. Yet it was not till some ten years later that he finally lost hope in the possibility of parliamentary reform and declared in favour of monarchy.

Although he must have had a foretaste during the Boer War and the events that led up to it of what he might expect to find when he became a Member of Parliament (for he condemned the attack on the Boers as a millionaires' ramp), yet the shock he received when he came face to face with parliamentary methods was a violent one. So violent that it gradually changed the whole focus of his energies from attempts (almost always nullified by the Executive) to redress specific injustices, to a concentrated attack upon the conduct of the Party system and the corruption of those who controlled it.

This change did not come immediately, for it took him some time to realize the extent and seriousness of the evils that were prevalent in the House of Commons. In his first two years as a Member the speeches he made and the questions he asked referred exclusively to disputed points of policy. He threw himself, for example, wholeheartedly into his Party's programme opposing the system of imported Chinese labour in the Transvaal mines. But in those first two years he learnt the difference between a programme and executive action. It was not until 1908 that he showed the first signs of rebellion against the way things were conducted by members of the House itself. This attack was directed against a practice which had in it the seeds of corruption—the secrecy under which political funds were accumulated and administered. It was an attack on a narrow front, but one which, had it been successful, would have opened the way to a more general probe into corrupt practices.

Belloc in his opening speech was at pains to emphasize the precise terms in which the motion was drawn. He admitted the need for political funds and went out of his way to make clear that he himself had had his parliamentary expenses paid out of the Liberal Party funds, and that no pressure of any sort had been brought to bear on him on the occasions when he had adopted an independent attitude. But he made a strong case against the secrecy attaching both to the origin and to the use of these funds, and urged that they should be publicly audited.

The House never divided on the motion. A red herring was drawn across its clear-cut issue by an amendment dealing with the particular activities of the Tariff Reform League, which let loose a whole spate of speeches on party lines. Whether or not this was intentionally introduced so as to kill the original motion cannot now be decided, but the fact remains that after the amendment had been accepted, the Speaker declined to allow the question contained in the main motion to be put, on the grounds that it was then after 11 p.m. The debate therefore stood adjourned.

This first probe into parliamentary proceedings was not followed up on the floor of the House with motions of a similar kind. Although during 1909 and 1910 Belloc was accumulating evidence that disgusted him of the ways governmental business was conducted and the hypocrisy of the party system, and though he kept up a sniping fire of pertinent questions which spared no party, he did not attack again, no doubt because he realized that any motion by a private member that laid Parliament open to serious outside criticism would be firmly quashed, as his motion on the political funds had been. He was coming to see that any attack, if it were to have a chance of success, must be made from outside Parliament. He did, however, make one more effort to get his views heard. At the general election in 1910 he stood as an independent candidate and was again elected by his constituents of South Salford. But he was soon convinced that, even in his non-party position, he would be unable to ventilate the evils he was determined to stamp out. At the end of the session he resigned and made a final speech (which Hansard thought fit to omit from its record) in which he told the House flatly what he thought of its methods and how he proposed to attack them as soon as he ceased to be a Member. He finished by saying that he had never left any place with so much pleasure as he felt in leaving the House of Commons. It was the speech of a rebel ready for action.

Action was not long delayed. In the summer of 1911 appeared the first issue of *The Eye Witness*, a weekly review, edited by Belloc, whose policy it was to tell the truth about the English political system as shown in its day-to-day working, and to bring under a searchlight of publicity the actions of Ministers. In September of the same year Belloc published, in conjunction with Cecil Chesterton, a scathing and fully documented attack upon the nature of English government under the title *The Party System*. In 1912 *The Servile State* made its appearance. In addition to these publications, which had the avowed object of stating in unambiguous language the hypocrisy and corruption existing in politics and of goading people into action, a stream of satirical novels poured from his pen pointing the same morals and bringing into derision and contempt the kind of men that the general public had been taught to look up to—Ministers of State and great financiers.

This was a new line of criticism in England and one which only a courageous reformer would have undertaken, for it attacked the most powerful forces in the State in matters that they particularly wished to be kept from the public eye. Moreover, the attack was pressed without quarter, and with a total disregard for the consequences it might have upon its author. For although Belloc has written 'To tell a particular truth with regard to a particular piece of corruption is of course, dangerous in the extreme; the rash man who might be tempted to employ this weapon would find himself bankrupted or in prison, and probably both', yet over and over again, and in one instance, the Marconi scandal, at the continued risk of undergoing exactly the penalties he names, he *did* tell particular truths with regard to particular pieces of corruption.

In this campaign Belloc found an able and equally courageous colleague in Cecil Chesterton. Besides collaborating with him in *The Party System* Chesterton was his right-hand man in the political work of *The Eye Witness*, and when Belloc relinquished the editorship at the end of a year, Chesterton took his place as editor and, fully supported by Belloc, continued the attack.

The nature of this attack upon the very fabric of the English parliamentary system and the social trends throughout the country was twofold. In *The Party System* it was directed, as we have seen, against the ways in which Parliament actually functioned and the corrupt practices it countenanced. In *The Servile State* an almost mathematical proof was set out, showing how capitalism must develop into a state of things in which the propertyless proletariat would be constrained by law to work for those in possession of the means of production. In other words the first part of the attack had as its driving force that the people of England were politically unfree; the second part, that the majority

43

were economically unfree, and, in a slightly different sense of the words, would be politically unfree also, since they would lack a free status in positive law. In both cases certain remedies were proposed. *The Eye Witness* (later under Cecil Chesterton's editorship called *The New Witness*) undertook to develop both elements of the attack week by week.

In the preface of *The Party System* the authors state that 'the object of this book is to support the tendency to expose and ridicule as it deserves, to destroy and supplant the system under which Parliament, the governing institution of this country, has been rendered null'. The main contention of the book is that the whole government of the country is directed and carried out by a clique of front bench Members from both sides of the House. This clique, which is recruited by co-option and whose composition—and even its existence—is kept secret, controls, not only all legislation, but also the management of elections, so that

> instead of the executive being controlled by the representative assembly, it controls it. Instead of the demands of the people being expressed for them by their representatives, the matters discussed by these representatives are settled by the very body which it is the business of the representative assembly to check and control.

This state of things, which had been developing during the previous half century, was made possible by the secret political funds collected and administered by the clique, funds whose collection and administration involved bribery on a large scale, at the one end by the sale of honours and lucrative posts, and at the other by rewarding those who were prepared to do the bidding of those in control. The book describes in detail the methods employed to prevent awkward motions, put down on the order paper by rebels against the system, from being discussed, and shows how it is practically impossible, at a general election as well as in the House, for so-called representatives—still less the people they are supposed to represent—either to initiate legislation or to criticize effectively any measure decided upon by the executive.

The manner of the book is forthright. Names of men in high office and alive at the time are given as examples of those who employ the

44

methods it condemns. Exactly how a great many of these, irrespective of Party, are related by birth or by marriage is meticulously recorded. Actual instances are given of the working of the system in the stifling of particular demands which, if given full play, would have interfered with the interests of wealthy patrons on whose financial support the clique relied.

The book is thus a gauntlet thrown down in challenge to the most powerful forces in the country. Its authors knew full well that in publishing it they were cutting themselves off from official support in any work they might take up thereafter. They were self-declared rebels against the comfortable conventions of the rulers. And yet, in spite of its courageous forthrightness, the book does not merely affirm, it studiously examines all the lines of defence that can be put forward for the system, and finally, when each of these arguments has been shown to be groundless, it attempts in the last chapter to answer the question 'Can the system be mended?' Here various remedies are proposed, such as the public audit of Party funds, and definite pledges to be extracted from candidates at an election that 'they would vote against the Government—whatever its composition—unless there were carried through the House of Commons, within a certain time, those measures to which they stood pledged'. But, no matter what remedies might be applied, Belloc and Chesterton were fully aware that no lasting reform could take place unless the people of the country could be awakened to political consciousness and to a resolution to make their will prevail. Political education of the democracy, by ruthlessly exposing the hypocrisies and corruption of government as it existed, was therefore the first purpose of the book. For although Belloc did not minimize the difficulties of getting an unpopular or unfamiliar truth accepted, he never ceased to believe that truth 'has this peculiar quality about it (which modern defenders of falsehood seem to have forgotten), that when it has been so much as suggested, it of its own self and by example tends to turn that suggestion into a conviction', for 'truth being fact, and therefore hard, must irritate and wound; but it has that power of growth and creation peculiar to itself which always makes it worth the telling'.

Belloc's rebellion, then, against political methods and political practices as he had seen them from inside Parliament, was prompted by his passionate desire for Truth and his hatred of corruption. He forfeited glittering material rewards by undertaking it. His campaign for social justice, as exemplified in *The Servile State*, *The Restoration of Property*, *Economics for Helen* and many pamphlets and speeches, though in its form a logical presentment of current tendencies and their consequences, was inspired by the same motives. In these latter treatises capitalism, with its progressive transformation into socialism, was shown to be the main enemy.

Here again the dice were loaded against him. The central thesis of *The Servile State*—that capitalism will be stabilized by the 'establishment of compulsory labour, legally enforceable upon those who do not own the means of production for the advantage of those who do' —was unacceptable to almost all sections of society; to the capitalist, because he claimed, though he was engineering the change, that the system under which he amassed riches was the enlightened economy of a free and prosperous country; to the wage-earner, because he imagined himself to be free and resented the suggestion that he was destined to become a slave; and to the community in general, because it had grown up with the idea that capitalism, which had brought England to a position of great wealth and power among the nations of the world, must be an ideal system and one of great stability. Belloc's line of argument therefore ran counter to the opinions of almost all his fellow-countrymen at the time he wrote. Once again he appears as the rebel reformer, battling against the strong current of vested interests, and, in this instance, of the delusions, too, of the populace as a whole. While most of his English readers took capitalism for granted, he held it up as an unstable system in process of dissolution; while socialists were evolving paper plans to go to what they believed to be the opposite extreme and introduce collectivism, he dubbed the latter a natural development of capitalism and one that would be equally unstable, unless forcibly introduced by means of confiscation; while the proletariat were priding themselves on their freedom to vote, he told them that their vote was meaningless and that their political freedom, which had already begun to disappear, would soon disappear altogether.

This attitude of rebellion against those in whose hands power resided —the banking monopoly, capitalism and controllers of Government— to say nothing of the deluded masses who had been taught to believe in them, had its inevitable effect upon his life. As we shall see in the next chapter, he came within an ace of charges which might have resulted in a prison sentence, and all through his career as a writer a strict boycott, not only of anything he might write himself, but even of any mention of his name or quotation from his work by other journalists, was ordered by certain proprietors of big daily papers whose methods he had condemned. There is no question about his passing the second and third tests, noted above, of the genuine reformer: he undoubtedly acted from a sense of justice and not from self-interest; and he took grave personal risks. But what of the other two tests? Were his accusations true, and did he offer constructive remedies?

As to the truth of his allegations in *The Party System*, that able critic, the late Edward Shanks, in a book written in conjunction with C. Creighton Manvell, writes:

> These truths [those exposed in *The Party System*] are today common knowledge. We all know that the power of government does not reside in practice with the people, but with some body which remains for most of us undefined. It is the peculiar service of the authors of *The Party System* to have defined that body for us and to have exposed its nature and composition.

Against the truth of Belloc's contention in *The Servile State* there have in recent years been several arguments put forward. The chief of these are: that the social tendency in the years since it was written has been towards State control and socialism and not, as he argued, towards a stabilization of the capitalist class by the legalized servitude of the proletariat. Secondly, that the first Insurance Act, which differentiated the class of owners from the class of non-owners, has been replaced by an Act applying to all classes alike.

It is true that the so-called 'nationalization' of certain major industries has developed to a greater extent than Belloc seemed to anticipate, but the methods adopted for buying out the capitalists have been

47

almost exactly those he described. The people who have suffered in this process are the taxpayers (that is to say, the population as a whole) and to some additional extent the shareholders in the nationalized industries. But this has not hit the capitalist class as such. The 'free enterprise' directors and manipulators of industrial companies are still in the saddle for the simple reason that the State, not being a business concern, cannot replace them with its own officials. Moreover the greater part of industry is still conducted by private enterprise on the same lines as before, except, as Belloc deduced from what he saw happening at the time of writing, that the non-owning class who sell their labour is far more strictly regimented and controlled than in 1912.

As to the present Insurance Act, which replaced the one Lloyd George put on the statute book, it is quite untrue to say that it has the effect of uniting the owning and non-owning classes in a single comprehensive schedule. There still remains the dividing line between employer and employee, in fact the differentiation has been accentuated by dispensing with the buffer friendly societies and by making universal the contributions by employers to the compulsory premiums taken from the employed. It is exactly what Belloc said would happen. When dealing with compulsory insurance he wrote:

> Dovetailing in with this machinery of compulsion is all that mass of registration and docketing which is accumulating through the use of Labour Exchanges. Not only will the Official have the power to enforce special contracts, or the power to coerce individual men to labour under the threat of a fine, but he will also have a series of *dossiers* by which the record of each workman can be established.

It would be as difficult to deny the truth of those words today as it would be to pretend that the proletariat was not more specially catered for and organized now than forty years ago, as a class having a special status different from the owning class and needing constant supervision by the State. Actually almost the only point that Belloc did not foresee is the present tendency of those in power to enlarge the number of proletarians by forcing professional men and small owners into a status of dependency. But *The Servile State* was not a prophecy. It was a logical deduction from social trends apparent in 1912.

It remains to outline the constructive reforms that Belloc advocated.

We have seen that in *The Party System* he tentatively suggested two reforms operative within the parliamentary system as organized—the auditing of Party funds and the exaction of special pledges from candidates at elections. By 1920 he had despaired of the effectiveness of these measures, even supposing that they could be brought about. He had come to look upon Parliament as an institution so effete and so permeated with corruption that the only way he could see of preserving the greatness and homogeneity of the nation was by a complete change in the form of government. In *The House of Commons and the Monarchy*, published in that year, he recommends that full executive powers should reside in the hands of a single person—a monarch—who should be held responsible for all laws promulgated and for all abuses that might arise. Subsidiary to the Monarch there were to be supporting Councils representing real interests, upon which he could rely and at the same time which he would control. He saw in the Trade Unions, in the legal, medical, and teaching professions, and in the police and national armed forces the embryo of such councils.

His arguments in favour of monarchy are concisely expressed and clear cut. An oligarchy is only tolerable when controlled by an aristocracy. Aristocracy as a controlling force in England is dead, or on the point of death, and aristocrats, once dead, cannot be brought to life again, nor can they acquire the democratic spirit. True democracy, in which citizens take part in their own government, is impossible in large modern States. Therefore monarchy remains the only solution, apart from chaos or a loss of independence. It is interesting to see in this argument how the principle underlying his republican views of earlier years remains the same in his advocacy of monarchy. That principle is egalitarianism—the conviction that men are equal, which he calls 'a mysterious, a religious dogma'—for, of egalitarian States, he writes, there are two forms: the actively democratic and the monarchic.

The solution which he proposes for our social problems is the Distributive State, one, that is to say, based upon a wide distribution of personal ownership. On this subject he has written frequently and at considerable length in *Restoration of Property*, *Economics for Helen*, and in countless articles.

Whatever opinions may be held about these constructive proposals, political and social, it must be admitted by everyone that he has upheld them with impartiality and logical exactness.

5 *The Marconi Scandal*

WHEN Belloc made his decision to leave the House of Commons and attack the evils he saw in it from outside, there was already maturing an example of these evils on an unprecedented scale. While he was yet a Member of Parliament—an independent now, freed from the constraints of the Party whip—events were happening which were to prove the forerunners of the greatest English parliamentary scandal on record.

On January 25th, 1910, Godfrey Isaacs was made managing director of the English Marconi Company. On March 7th Sir Rufus Isaacs was made Solicitor General, and in October was promoted to the office of Attorney General. Somewhat later, but before the scandal broke upon the world, Lloyd George had become Chancellor of the Exchequer and Murray, Master of Elibank, Chief Whip of the Liberal Party. These men were to be the principal actors in the Marconi drama.

It is an extraordinary story, not merely because high Government officials were concerned (there have been scandals of a similar kind at one time or another in the governments of most countries) but for two special reasons. First, because, in spite of the publicity the affair received and in spite of a Parliamentary Committee's 2,000-page report on it, a great many facts, essential to a full understanding of it, were left unexamined; and secondly, because two of the men had signal honours heaped upon them. One occupied the post of Lord Chief Justice and later that of Viceroy of India, and the second became Prime Minister.

If I tell this story again (and I dare say many of the present generation have never heard it), it is in order to establish two facts: that there was ample justification for Belloc's campaign against governmental practices, and that he ran grave personal risks in conducting it.

Here then is the story in outline.

In the early months of 1910 a Government Committee, known as the Cables (Landing Rights) Committee, was considering the establishment of a State-owned system of wireless stations throughout the Empire. To this Committee there came in March an application from the English Marconi Company (whose managing director was Godfrey Isaacs) for licences to establish eighteen wireless stations. No action was taken by the Committee for a year. Then on March 18th, 1911, it received a memo from the Post Office to the effect that a State-owned service was inadvisable because the Marconi Company would not be satisfied with a Government service equipped with their apparatus, their object being to have a service of their own. This memo gives the impression that the Marconi Company had no rivals who could do the work and therefore it was better to humour them. Actually, only ten days later the Admiralty submitted a scheme for a State-owned system which the chairman of the Committee wished to recommend to the Government; and in October of the same year the Poulsen Company also submitted a scheme.

On March 7th the Marconi Company's scheme was accepted by the Post Office, in spite of the fact that certain important figures in it had been found to be incorrect, and that its terms were much less advantageous to the Government than were those of the two other schemes submitted. This decision had of course to be approved by the House of Commons, and the Marconi contract was laid on the table of the House on July 19th. It is between these two dates, March 7th and July 19th, that the main drama of the Marconi scandal was enacted, a drama the facts of which remained unrevealed for some five months, and were then only partially made known.

The story of what happened between these two crucial dates is as follows. Besides the English Marconi Company there existed an American Marconi Company, more than half of whose shares were held by the English Company. Godfrey Isaacs was a director of both, and before the granting of the contract the shares of both companies were at a low ebb. As soon as Isaacs learned that his tender had been accepted, he circularized the news amongst shareholders of the English Company, but omitted to mention a clause in the contract which gave the Government the right to substitute any rival system whenever it saw fit. This naturally caused the shares of the Company to rise rapidly. This done, he set off to America. His first action there was to buy up the assets of the United Wireless Company (the Marconi Company's principal rival in the United States) and sell them to the American Marconi Company at a considerable profit. He then persuaded the latter company to increase its capital by the issue of 1,400,000 five-dollar shares (five dollars was at that time equivalent to £1 1s. 3d. in English money), and he made himself personally responsible for the placing of 500,000 of these shares. He thus not only raised the prestige of the American Company (a letter of congratulation from his brother Rufus, the Attorney General, helped him considerably in this), but also linked it still more closely with the English Company. By April 9th he was back in England with the 500,000 shares, not yet publicly authorized, in his possession.

He lost no time. On April 9th he invited his two brothers Rufus and Harry to lunch and gave them the opportunity of buying as many shares as they wished at £1 1s. 3d. Harry took 50,000 but Rufus declined to buy direct from Godfrey, the Managing Director of the Company that had just received a Government contract. However, on April 17th he bought 10,000 from Harry at £2 apiece, and on the same day sold 1,000 each to Lloyd George and Murray at the same price. Two days later on April 19th the American shares were officially put on the market for the first time at £3 5s. per share. This price rose to £4 by the evening of the same day. On that day Rufus sold 7,000 of his remaining shares on the open market at an average price of £3 6s. 6d. a share, and Murray bought for the Liberal Party Fund 2,500. The next day Lloyd George and Murray each sold 500 at £3 3s. On May 14th Murray bought 500 more for the Party Fund, and on the 19th he and Lloyd George added 1,500 more to their private buyings at £2 3s. per share.

Now there are several points to notice about these transactions. First, that three Ministers of the Crown (all of them in influential positions) were involved in deals which from a purely financial point of view were highly irregular and, on the political level, could hardly fail to rouse the suspicion that the Ministers in question had used their positions in the Government to create a situation in which they would be able to enrich themselves. For, secondly, a brother of one of them.

who was a Managing Director of the Company that had just been given a very large Government contract, was the seller of these shares to the Ministers *before* they could be bought on the open market and consequently, at a price far below the actual market price on the opening day. And, thirdly, that there is no record of the sale of these shares to Ministers at the outset, for they were negotiated privately, without brokers, between the Ministers and Godfrey Isaacs, or, to be strictly accurate, between the Ministers and Harry Isaacs acting as a go-between with them and Godfrey. The only record is of the 7,000 shares sold on the open market by Rufus Isaacs on the day the market opened. The account of the rest of the transactions depends for its authenticity solely upon the statement of Rufus Isaacs' Counsel belatedly made in March 1913.

That was the first act in the drama, which may be said to have ended on May 22nd, 1912, when, as far as can be ascertained, Ministerial gambling ceased. It was an act played behind a lowered curtain. There were, however, some holes in the curtain through which a few enterprising journalists and finance experts in the City had been peeping. The result of this peeping was that when the curtain was raised for the first time with the stage set for the second act, questions began to be asked.

When the Marconi contract was laid on the table of the House of Commons, there was a general outcry at its terms, which were extremely favourable to the Company. It provided that the Company should receive a 10 per cent. royalty on gross receipts for a period of twenty-eight years; that, in spite of the fact that it possessed only two unexpired patents, one of which expired in 1914 and the other in 1918. Moreover, the Admiralty and Poulsen schemes had contracted to erect stations at a cost of £36,000 less per station than the Marconi Company. But in addition to the favourable terms of the contract, there were rumours everywhere, not only in the City but in the United States and Canada as well, that three Ministers had been making fortunes in gambling with the shares of a Company to which a brother of one of them had persuaded the Government to give a contract.

In these circumstances it was decided not to hurry the contract through Parliament on the last day of the session but to debate the

Belloc in 1912

whole question early in the next. In this debate, held on October 11th, Rufus Isaacs and Lloyd George made statements calculated to deceive the House without actually perjuring themselves. The line taken by them was to deny the purchase of any shares in the company to which the contract had been given. They made no mention whatever of the American Marconi Company (and their dealings with it) though the prices of the latter's shares were governed by the fortunes of the English Company. The Master of Elibank was not present. He had gone to South America where he remained until the whole affair had blown over. A Parliamentary Committee of Inquiry was, however, promised and began to take evidence shortly after.

This Committee's report, which was not issued till nearly five months later, has been sometimes used as an argument to show that the actors in the Marconi drama, though imprudent—even improper—in some of their actions, had acted in good faith. That was indeed the interpretation put upon it in a final debate on the subject in the House of Commons. Actually the evidence given before the Committee constitutes one of the most damning indictments of the Ministers concerned that could well be imagined. It is also a damning indictment of those responsible for the report itself, for over and over again they refused to pursue lines of inquiry into the conduct of the Ministers that had been opened up in the evidence, thus avoiding the possibility of outright condemnation of them.

Here I cannot do more than refer to one or two points in the evidence—out of the very many that could be cited—which bear this out.

Of the three Ministers concerned in the buying and selling of shares it is only necessary to say that their evidence was not taken by the Parliamentary Committee until nearly five months after it had begun proceedings, and that during all that time it was generally assumed that they would substantiate what they had implied in the debate of October 11th—namely that they had bought no shares. But a few days before they were called to give evidence a curious incident occurred. The French paper *Le Matin* published an account, wholly without foundation, purporting to be a summary of the evidence given by Mr Leo Maxse before the Committee the day before. This article reported Mr Maxse as saying that Rufus Isaacs and Godfrey Isaacs had bought shares in the English Marconi Company at 50 francs before the contract was accepted, and sold them at 200 francs afterwards. Mr Maxse had said nothing of the kind, but he *had* introduced for the first time in the proceedings the question of Ministerial gambling in *American* Marconis, and the raising of the question must have warned Rufus Isaacs that his prevarications in the October debate would now be seen for what they were. He therefore seized the opportunity of bringing a libel action against *Le Matin*, and though the latter had withdrawn the charge and apologized, he insisted on making a statement through his Counsel—without the risks of cross-examination—in which he admitted his dealings in the shares of the American Company. Whether or not the *Matin's* 'blunder' (it is extremely difficult to account for it seeing that Mr Maxse's evidence was published for all to see) was deliberately arranged by Rufus Isaacs so that he could make his admission in the least unfavourable circumstances possible, we cannot be sure. But what is certain is that 'he happened to be in Paris' when the libel was printed.

A few days later Rufus Isaacs and Lloyd George (Lord Murray was still away in South America and, in spite of a summons to give evidence before the Committee, remained there undisturbed) were called to give evidence before the Parliamentary Committee and they were naturally questioned on their dealings in American Marconis and asked why they had not admitted this in the parliamentary debate. Rufus Isaacs answered that obviously these dealings could have no bearing on the rumours that were circulating, so he did not mention them. Lloyd George merely said that there was no time that afternoon; and, since two Ministers had spoken, he did not feel justified in taking up more of the House's time. Both these answers were of course wholly unsatisfactory, for the American Company was so closely linked to the English Company that the rise of the shares of the former was mainly due to the contract obtained by the latter and as to the time allotted to the debate, it is farcical to suppose that Lloyd George could not have found time in a speech full of recrimination against the 'sinister rumours passing from one foul lip to another behind the backs of the House' to mention his dealings in American Marconis. But unsatisfactory though these answers were, the Ministers were not pressed further.

And now we come to the Parliamentary Committee and the way in which its proceedings were conducted. It consisted of fifteen members, nine chosen from the Liberal majority in the House and six from the Conservative Opposition. Examination of the proceedings shows that whatever effective cross-examination there was of the Ministers' evidence, and whatever suggestions for pressing it home, came from the Conservative minority, and was invariably nullified by the Liberal majority. The Liberal members showed an unbroken front for the protection of their political leaders.

The first thing to note about the proceedings of the Committee is the order in which they took the evidence. Instead of calling first the Ministers whose conduct was in question, and whose evidence presumably would have gone far to clearing up one aspect of the inquiry, the Committee left them alone for five months, and only then called them, as I have shown, after the question of gambling in American Marconis, introduced by Mr Maxse, made this inevitable. Actually the first witness was Sir Alexander King, Permanent Secretary to the Post Office. His evidence cannot be said to have done anything to exonerate the Ministers concerned. When asked about the Admiralty scheme sent to Cables (Landing Rights) Committee, he replied: 'The Admiralty put in a scheme which the Committee approved, at least the Chairman said he approved. Later, the Post Office put in a scheme which the Committee accepted. Why they changed their minds I do not know.' Again, dealing with the contract, he mentioned concessions made to the Government by the Marconi Company, also important conversations that took place and letters that passed, but could produce no record of any of these occurrences. Furthermore, he admitted that no technical advice had been sought to test the value of the Marconi Company. If the Parliamentary Committee took note of these admissions, they do not appear to have attached any weight to them.

The next evidence to be taken was from journalists who had discussed the Marconi affair. The attitude of the Committee towards these witnesses was like that of a Prosecuting Counsel cross-examining a prisoner in a criminal trial. These methods affected witnesses in different ways. Belloc and Leo Maxse, for example, stood up to them and refused to be led into traps, but W. R. Lawson, a member of the Stock

Exchange and an experienced writer on financial matters, whose cross-examination lasted for four or five days, was obviously confused by the verbal battering he was receiving and was forced into admissions quite contrary to the general purport of the articles he had written and (it may be presumed) the opinions he really held. Almost every sentence of his articles in *The Outlook* was subjected to a microscopic examination, and the general meaning and factual accuracy of what he had written was covered up by refusal to allow common-sense explanation. Some of the other journalists fared better. Belloc, who was called to answer questions about articles he had written for *The New Witness*, while stating that he had written a great deal on the subject, categorically refused to reveal which particular articles were from his pen, making it clear that Cecil Chesterton, the editor, wished to be held entirely responsible for everything that appeared in his paper. His cross-examination by Mr Booth affected him so little that in another place he described it as 'pitiful.' Leo Maxse, editor of *The National Review*, also refused to be bullied. Every effort was made by the Committee (even including the threat of a prison sentence) to force him to reveal the names of those people who had given him information in confidence of what was going on. Neither persuasion nor threats moved him from the position he had taken up—namely, refusal to break his word to those who had trusted him as an editor. The threats were not carried out, and he was not recalled.

But perhaps the most significant evidence given by the journalists came from Mr Powell, the acting editor of the *Financial News*. He stated that opinion in the City was that a large and powerful syndicate was responsible for the whole of the Marconi operations, and that among its members were men of high position. He went on to say that one of the most pointed reports was that an account was opened on the syndicate's behalf at a certain bank and swelled in a few days, by means of brokers' cheques, to about £70,000. Then the person who had originally opened the account came and attempted to draw practically the whole amount in five- and ten-pound notes, which seemed to suggest a desire for concealment of the dealings. Powell gave the name of the banker so that the Committee might summon him and test the story. If this report had been sifted it seems likely that it would have revealed much more extensive gambling in shares than was ever admitted by Isaacs, and would have cleared the way for an accurate judgement by the Committee. But no action was taken, and the personnel of the syndicate was never brought to light.

When at last the Committee decided (one might almost say, was forced by the introduction into Leo Maxse's evidence of the possibility of gambling by Ministers in the shares of the *American* Marconi Company) to examine the Ministers and Godfrey Isaacs, the whole tone of the proceedings changed. Instead of acting, as they did in the case of the journalists, like Counsel for the Prosecution, members of the Committee appeared for the most part in the light of advocates on behalf of the witnesses. Neither Rufus Isaacs nor Lloyd George was pressed to give reasons for the statements they made or to substantiate them. One of the central points to be cleared up was whether and, if so, to what extent, the shares in the American Company, in which these Ministers had gambled before they came officially onto the market, were influenced by what was happening to the English Company. Rufus Isaacs and Lloyd George both denied categorically that they were influenced in any way. This, in spite of the sharp rise in the American shares after the Government contract had been given to the English Company; in spite of the fact that three directors of the English Company were also directors of the American Company; and in spite of the large number of shares held by the English Company in the American Company. To some extent the Conservative members of the Committee did attempt, through cross-examination, to get from the Ministers an explanation of the grounds on which they based their denials. But it was a half-hearted attempt, constantly interrupted by objections from the Liberal contingent to the questions put. A second vital question was of course whether the decision of the Post Office to give the contract to the Marconi Company was in any way influenced by either of two facts: that the Attorney General was a brother of that company's Managing Director, or that opportunities were presented to both the Attorney General and the Chancellor of the Exchequer for profitable gambling in the shares of the American Company owing to the negotiations that took place in America immediately after the signing of the contract. Such a suggestion was strongly denied by both these Ministers and by the Postmaster General, and there the matter was allowed to drop. Perhaps the general attitude of the Committee may be summed up in the Chairman's remark to Rufus Isaacs at the conclusion of his evidence: 'We thank you for the very frank way in which you have given your evidence, and I am only sorry we have had to keep you so long.' Nothing of that kind was said to Mr Lawson, although his cross-examination had lasted two or three times as long as Rufus Isaacs', and his evidence, to say the least, was equally frank.

From these few instances of the manner in which the work of the Committee was conducted, its inaction where the reputation of Ministers was involved, and its final majority report entirely whitewashing them, it must, I think be clear that the truth—whatever it may exactly have been—was deliberately withheld. The final debate in Parliament on this report followed the accustomed line of party politics. A Conservative motion 'that this House regrets the transactions of certain of its Ministers in the shares of the Marconi Company of America, and the want of frankness displayed by Ministers in their communications on the subject to the House', was duly defeated by 346 (Government supporters) as against 268 Conservatives.

That in brief outline is the story of the Marconi scandal. Its importance, so far as Belloc is concerned, consists in its bearing upon his views on inter-party front bench collusion and the prevalence of corrupt practices in Parliament. As regards corruption, it is inconceivable, even from the fragments of evidence that the Parliamentary Committee allowed to come to light, that so vast a column of smoke as that which enveloped the City and spread across the sea to America could have arisen without fire. Indeed the fire is there for all to see in the Ministerial admissions. The only question to be answered is the extent of the corruption. It still cannot be said with certainty why the wireless contract was given to the Marconi Company, or to what length Ministerial gambling went. But it was exactly these dark places that Belloc and Chesterton set out to illuminate, and there was only one way in which they could hope to succeed. That was by making such damaging personal accusations against the Ministers as to force them to defend themselves against their accusers. It was in this that the attack by *The New Witness* differed from all other comments on the case (for there is all the difference in the world between calling a particular man a swindler and complaining that the case against the Ministers ought to be sifted more thoroughly) and it was by this personal attack that its writers laid themselves open to criminal proceedings. The fact that no libel action was brought against Belloc or Chesterton (the latter's trial in 1913 was the result of a quite different attack) goes far to show that the Ministers feared what new disclosures might be extracted from them under cross-examination, in other words, that the accusations could not be satisfactorily answered.

Another result of this refusal by the Ministers to be stung into action was of course that Belloc failed to get a public verdict against them. But there are indications that a trial was very nearly staged. At least two of his closest friends, who were in a position to know what was going on, were so worried by the risks he was running that they did everything they could to dissuade him from persisting in his attack. There was also a curious incident, which may or may not have had a bearing on the Ministers' decision to take no action. Belloc and his wife were invited, at the moment when action seemed most likely, to pass the week-end at the country house of Mr Justice Darling. Belloc, rightly or wrongly, felt that his own grasp of the facts and his ability to marshal them in a way that would have brought disgrace not only to the Ministers themselves but to the whole Party that was defending them was being tested. If this surmise was correct, Mr Justice Darling must have given it as his opinion that action was too dangerous.

So much for corruption. As regards collusion between the two front benches of the House, it has been argued that, since both the report of the Parliamentary Committee and the debate that finally absolved the Ministers achieved their results strictly in accordance with the strength of the two political Parties—the Liberal majority in each instance being the deciding factor—Belloc's theory of collusion between the two Parties was disproved. But such an argument is based on a misunderstanding of what Belloc said. He never suggested that there was collusion between all Members of Parliament on the Government side and all those of the Opposition. Collusion, according to him, existed between a clique of *front bench* Members on each side of the House.

This, in order to be effective and to preserve the illusion of a battle between the two Parties, had to be conducted secretly and the House as a whole had to be encouraged to vote on strictly Party Lines. What happened in the Marconi case followed exactly the pattern of procedure that Belloc had exposed. The inter-Party front bench clique decided that exposure of the Ministers was to be avoided at all costs, for that would have struck a fatal blow at the prestige of parliamentary government throughout the country. The thing was on too big a scale to be dealt with by selecting a scapegoat. Therefore the Ministers must be whitewashed, and this was done quite simply by ensuring that the Government supporters, always in a majority, should back up their leaders. Conservative Members, though mildly critical, as was shown by Lord Robert Cecil's unadopted report on the Committee, were kept within safe bounds by Balfour's declaration that he did not intend to make Party capital out of the incident.

There can, I think, be little doubt by any impartial observer that Belloc's accusations against parliamentary procedure are borne out by the Marconi scandal, and the very fact that the Ministers involved escaped scot free and later rose to some of the highest positions in the State shows how strong was the power of the anonymous clique that controlled the whole business of government and against which Belloc unavailingly fought. Little wonder after this trial of strength that he came to the conclusion that only by a complete change in the form of government could the political destiny of England be put on a sound footing.

To complete this story it remains to say a word about Cecil Chesterton's trial for criminal libel on an action brought against him by Godfrey Isaacs. The line taken by Chesterton, which led up to this trial, was strongly opposed by Belloc. It consisted in hunting up and publishing, with highly disparaging comments in *The New Witness*, the previous companies that Godfrey Isaacs had either promoted or taken part in as a director. Every one of these companies had failed and much money had been lost by shareholders. Chesterton's argument was that here was a matter of fraudulent dealings whereby money was made for the promoter and directors at the expense of ignorant shareholders. The reason that he gave for bringing to public notice Godfrey Isaacs' past dealings and presenting them in as damaging a light as possible was that that was the only way of bringing one of the actors in the Marconi drama into court and subjecting him to cross-examination.

It is possible that his statement before the magistrate at Bow Street that he was going to justify at his trial the attacks that had appeared in *The New Witness* may have been a factor in Rufus Isaacs' decision to bring a writ against *Le Matin* and admit his dealings in American Marconis. For the writ was delivered two days after Chesterton's statement at Bow Street; but there cannot be any certainty about this, for, as we have seen, Maxse's evidence before the Parliamentary Committee had been enough to bring things to a head. Whatever the cause, the admission had been made, and in such a way that the damaging effects of it had been minimized, *before* Chesterton's trial. The latter's courage in risking a prison sentence for the sake of extracting damning admissions from the Isaacs brothers at the trial was therefore largely wasted. He suffered too under cross-examination, for though he persisted in his accusation of abominable conduct by Godfrey Isaacs, he was forced into a position with regard to Rufus Isaacs in which he had either to accuse him of perjury without definite proof, or else abandon his charge against him of dishonest and dishonourable conduct. He abandoned the charge.

The jury brought in a verdict of guilty, and the judge imposed a fine of £100 and costs on Chesterton. This was an unexpectedly light sentence for one found guilty of criminal libel, but the fact remains that this final attempt to bring hidden points of the Marconi case into the open failed in its purpose. Belloc had realized that this concentration on a side issue was a mistake and had done his best to dissuade Chesterton from taking the steps that led to the trial. Of the central scandal it can only be said that those who controlled Parliament were strong enough to ward off the attack that came so near to disgracing important Ministers of the Crown and the House of Commons itself.

6 Belloc and the Faith

BELLOC, when asked why it was that so many public lavatories in England were built underground, replied that this was ultimately due to the Reformation, leaving his questioner to puzzle out the line of argument. This answer, though surprising, was typical of his strong conviction that religion was the prime moulder of men's actions, and hence of events and institutions. Pick up almost any of his books and you will find, before you have read many pages, some reference, direct or indirect, to men's beliefs and the conflicting dogmas to which they subscribe. He saw the world, not as a conglomeration of races and disparate individuals, but as a place in which men and women fall into two groups: on the one hand those who had received the gift of faith and knowledge of the truth; and on the other those who pursue a medley of will-o'-the-wisps, each deviating in one way or another from truth, and hence deceptive and harmful.

That conviction coloured all his writing, or at all events all that he wrote after his marriage; for, as we have seen when discussing *The Path to Rome*, it was the influence of his wife that caused him to re-examine and grasp anew the Faith in which he had been baptized. Even without reading his books oneself it would be impossible not to realize the primacy of the Faith in his scale of values. Not once but many times I have heard the remark, 'Belloc is such a fine writer. What a pity it is that he is always harping on religion.' He is indeed always harping on religion. It is for him the one great motive power of the world, the touchstone that distinguishes truth from falsehood, chaos from order.

It would then be inexcusable, even in this slight testimony to his greatness as a man and a writer, to omit what is the central core of his life and his work.

As I have said, almost all of his books touch in one way or another upon the Faith he held, but certain of them deal more specifically with it. These latter fall into three main classes: those that recount episodes in the history of the Church through the centuries, such as *How the Reformation Happened*, *The Great Heresies*, *Survivals and New Arrivals*, and *The Crisis of Our Civilization*; those that explain and extol the nature and manifestations of the Faith in the world, notably *Europe and the Faith*, but also many shorter essays; and one, *The Question and the Answer*, addressed to the unbeliever, which sets out the grounds for belief in what the Catholic Church teaches.

In the first group of historical surveys there is a general thesis running through them all, repeated in each book with only differences of detail and emphasis according to the particular subject under examination. He tells the story of the Church's early struggles and persecutions; the official recognition of the Faith under Constantine; the power and unifying influence of the Roman Empire; the growth of Christendom through the Dark Ages, though always under the threat of dissolution from hostile forces within and without; the religious unity of the thirteenth century; the Great Schism, the anti-Popes, the disastrous consequences of the Black Death, which prepared the ground for the catastrophe of the Reformation; and last of all the Reformation itself and its fruits. The whole is told with the clarity and force of a logical mind permeated by the conviction that Europe—and, from Europe, the world—owes its civilization to the Church and the transcendental dogmas of the Catholic Faith. That, as we have seen, is the unifying principle underlying the whole of his historical writings, but in these books, specifically designed to show the inseparable relationship that exists between Europe and the Faith that formed her, not only is the divine source of her mission explained, but all the literary, artistic, and scientific achievements of the centuries are brought under scrutiny and, as it were, fitted into the divine scheme of things. They are the accidents, sometimes misused, of a civilization whose substance is elsewhere.

But the mark of all these books is the application of an indestructible principle to the myriad events and changes of history, and on whatever subject Belloc is setting out to write he contrives to show the immediate importance at the present time of decisions arrived at and actions taken long ago. For history to him is never merely an academic study of the past, but much more like a living being—immortal while

65

time lasts—whose character, action, talents, and excesses remain constant and continue their varying influences and effects throughout the centuries; a being endowed with free will, yet under the guidance and protection of a supernatural power, so that when it errs, it comes into conflict with that which governs it, and thus warps its own nature until expiation has been made and counter-action taken.

An example of this attitude to history may be found in *The Great Heresies*. It might well be thought that for modern readers heresy is a term now quite out of date, and that anything written thereon could be of no more than academic interest. Belloc is quick to contradict any such idea. After defining heresy as 'the dislocation of some complete and self-supporting scheme by the introduction of a novel denial of some essential part therein', he proceeds to show that by leaving standing a great part of the structure it attacks, heresy can appeal to believers the more effectively, and yet at the same time vitally change the nature of their belief and originate a new life of its own. In a word, where religion is concerned, it is one of the most potent solvents of civilizations. Though the average man rarely uses the word heresy in its true sense, and though many of the great heresies of the past are now dead, yet others persist—such as Islam and Protestantism—while others again of a more general kind are coming to birth.

In this way Belloc at once puts his subject into a present day setting. For example when writing of the Arian Heresy which made such inroads into the Church in the fourth and fifth centuries, he shows the probable changes that would have resulted in the history and way of life of Europeans if it had been successful in its attempt to rationalize a part of the Church's teaching. In a similar but reverse way he points out the social, political, and domestic changes that Protestantism has brought to England and estimates the differences that would be apparent if the Reformation had not taken place. This is all part of his sense of history as a single living entity, changing in the same way as a man changes during his life, but remaining always the same person, though marked by the vicissitudes of the past.

In all his surveys of particular crises in the Church's history his arguments are always developed against a background of opinion opposed to his own. Thus in *How the Reformation Happened* he is at

66

pains to state the case, first, of the Protestant, and, secondly, of the sceptical or atheist historian.

To the man of Protestant culture [he writes] the process leading to the Reformation seems obvious. From a variety of causes, knowledge vastly expanded at the close of the Middle Ages. Geographical discoveries followed each other rapidly and on a new scale of greatness; a true idea was acquired of the earth and heavens; arts improved; at the same time antiquity was rediscovered; original manuscripts were closely examined; a science of history began. The period is known as 'The Renaissance', the New Birth of Europe. Under such an influence the myths of a thousand uncritical years were exposed and dissolved. The institutions founded on these myths (the Papacy, the Mass, reliance on imagined influences of shrine and relic) were sapped, and with them crumbled all the society they informed.

That is, I think, a very fair summary of the Protestant view, if we add certain blots in the administration of the Church, which Belloc elsewhere is the first to admit. Equally fair and realistic is his description of the attitude of the sceptic.

To these men Catholicism seems a phase of thought present among their ancestry, natural to their blood, creative in its day, but now exposed as demonstrably false. It lamely survives today—principally in women—through a mere adhesion to traditional and homely things. It is also supported politically (but without conviction) by those who act from affection for the past, from fear of disorder, or from mere interest. Its life, however, has departed. The Church is a corpse.

Against this background he erects the majestic figure of the Church Universal, the creator of our civilization, the pearl of great price. The arguments of his opponents appear paltry in face of the thing they have lost—a thing continuing, resplendent, immortal, because it is divine, the maker of Europe and the hope of the world.

At first sight *Europe and the Faith*, which I have placed in a separate category from the books, just discussed, which elaborate certain episodes

67

in the history of the Church, would appear to be just another of the same kind, somewhat more detailed perhaps and of wider scope, but essentially similar. In both there is an historical setting that relates the material achievements of the Roman Empire to the divinely inspired message of the Church. In both the victories and set-backs of the Faith are vividly described. But nevertheless *Europe and the Faith* stands out as something *sui generis*. For whereas the other books I have mentioned have as their main object to examine particular challenges that the Church has met from the earliest times to the present day, *Europe and the Faith* is an impassioned avowal, and at the same time a fully reasoned defence, of the dictum with which the book finishes: 'The Faith is Europe, and Europe is the Faith.' It views European history since the Christian era as a whole and identifies the civilization that springs from Europe with the rise and continuing influences of the Church. Ancient Greece laid the intellectual and artistic foundations upon which the edifice was to be built, and Rome—especially Imperial Rome—provided the terrain and the architectural skill necessary for the building, but it was the Church that re-created and completed the work of its forerunners, inspiring it with a spirit that fulfils—and is alone in fulfilling—the high destiny and ultimate desires of mankind.

Considerable exception has been taken to the declaration I have quoted above, 'The Faith is Europe, and Europe is the Faith.' It is argued that though the Faith may have made Europe, yet it cannot be identified with it to the exclusion of the rest of the world. Such a statement would conflict with the universality which the Church claims. This argument is, I think, based on a misunderstanding of Belloc's meaning. Obviously he had no intention of confining the Faith within the boundaries of a single continent. That would have been absurd and a denial of Catholicism. What his incisive words imply is, first, that the soul of Europe—the form of her very existence—was fashioned by, and found its fulfilment in, the Catholic Church; and secondly, that in that centre and home of the Faith (strikingly identified with the Faith itself) the message was to be sought by the rest of the world. It is a bold and confident pronouncement, but one which the whole of his book was written to clarify and reinforce.

With such a lofty theme in view and one that was at the very core of his being, it is not surprising that in *Europe and the Faith* Bellocs' writing takes on a style of concentrated energy and personal avowal of the mysteries of the Faith rarely equalled in his other books. He returns over and over again to his central contention with a wealth of new similes and images, strikingly illuminating the main points of his thesis. Facts of history, often little known to the average reader, are diligently explored and their results recorded; the flow and ebb of the Faith in different periods are accurately assessed with their consequences in the life of Europeans; the continuing framework of Imperial Rome, weakened but not demolished, is pictured as supporting novel experiments in internal construction, and above all as depending for its stability on the strength of the new material of the Faith that had come to reinforce it; but perhaps the most remarkable thing about the book is the occasional lifting of the curtain of Belloc's personal reserve. In his white-hot determination to establish his thesis he allows the reader now and then to catch glimpses of his more intimate thoughts.

No, *Europe and the Faith* cannot be put into the same class as those other books which deal with different aspects of the history of the Church in Europe. It is at once more complete in its survey and more insistent upon the vital importance of its message. It is a vision and an exhortation even more than the exposition of a closely-knit argument.

The other book I have noted as being one of those specifically dealing with the Faith—*The Question and the Answer*—is of a quite different kind from all the others. It is an essay in philosophy, addressed to the sceptic, in which Belloc sets out to show the grounds for belief in the Catholic Church and its teaching. As in all his books he manifests an individual approach to his subject. His own mind, as we have seen and as he has often himself stated, was cast in a sceptical mould. He had a high regard for human reason and was by nature disinclined to accept the testimony of others. Thus he had a certain affinity with the intelligent exponents of atheism. He understood their arguments because he had felt the force of them himself, and in this book he is not so much a teacher as a disciplined explorer into the realms of truth. We cannot help feeling as we read his lucid enunciation of the arguments brought against the validity of the existence of God, and more especially those countering the claims of the Catholic Church, that his own difficulties in fully accepting the Faith were, generally speaking, caused by just such arguments. That he *did* accept it in its entirety and make it the mainspring of all his actions is of course undeniable, but that he had gone through a fierce mental struggle before arriving at certitude seems equally certain. The very boldness of his probing into the sources of disbelief is, I think, a proof of both these facts. It certainly adds greatly to the appeal he makes to other sceptical minds.

From all this it follows that *The Question and the Answer* is not so much a handbook of Catholic philosophy as a personal vindication of the faith the author holds, supported indeed by the basic arguments of St Thomas Aquinas but adapted throughout to the particular types of modern mind with which Belloc had come in contact and whose errors and shortcomings he had set himself to correct. For instance, in the first part, in which he is concerned with truths that can be attained by human reason, he passes over the Thomistic proofs of the existence of God derived from 'a First Mover' and 'The Efficient Cause' as being unlikely to convince the modern mind, and puts forward as his chief argument that based upon the axiom that *ex nihilo nihil fit*. Nor does he altogether escape criticism from the theologians in some of his statements, notably the one in which he sets the proof of personal immortality beyond the scope of human reason.

But in spite of (perhaps because of) the personal character of the book and, maybe, its occasional defects in the eyes of a philosopher, it provides a closely reasoned and eminently fair presentment of the case that he is arguing. As always he shows himself to be a master of vivid similes that clarify and enliven the points he is making, and he never shirks a difficulty or allows his arguments to become confused. This facing of a difficulty is especially noticeable in the second part of the book, entitled 'The Witness of Revelation'. To a logical mind like Belloc's the truths that can be reached by the human reason naturally present less difficulty than those that depend upon supernatural revelation for their substantiation. But as a Catholic he fully realizes that 'natural religion', that is, a religion confined to the discoveries made by the reason alone, is not enough. In his own words:

Natural religion is not sufficient for man. This does not mean that

Lithograph of Belloc by Daphne Pollen (1934)

it does not procure him ecstatic bliss (for it obviously does not do that), but rather that it does not even procure him so much satisfaction as leaves him free from heavy preoccupation upon his nature and doom, and the nature of the universe.

Accordingly the second part of his book is devoted to an inquiry whether or not there exists evidence of a special revelation given by God to mankind which establishes further fundamental truths, truths sufficient to answer satisfactorily the greatest of all questions, 'What am I?' It is therefore an examination of the credentials the witness of such a revelation must possess if it is to be accepted as trustworthy. His procedure is not unlike that of a barrister cross-examining a witness in court, pouncing upon all weak spots in the evidence and excluding pronouncements based upon undefined opinion or unsupported documents. Or perhaps it would be more accurate to compare his method to the summing up of a case by a judge in which he distinguishes between reliable and unreliable evidence. He is here again adopting the position of the sceptic, but with the big difference that he has discovered a witness that bears all the marks of truth and which cannot be shaken by rational questioning. He concludes the book with these words:

> In point of fact there is not on earth any other thing, body, institution, or person bearing all these marks at once save the Catholic Church . . . the perception of their actual existence, together with other motives of credibility, affords to much the most of those who accept her as the unique Witness a sufficient ground for such acceptance.

His arguments from beginning to end are thus those of the rational mind seeking an increase of knowledge. He does not, for example, specifically discuss the nature of faith, that it is a Divine gift, though of course he accepted the definition, but rather concerned himself with giving rational grounds for the acceptance of that gift.

In these books that I have selected to exemplify Belloc's attitude to the Catholic Church the historical and logical aspects of the Faith are, as we have seen, especially prominent. That is only to be expected by anyone acquainted with the quality of his mind. There is the same background to most of his work. All his economic and sociological writing, for example, bears the same marks, and his purely descriptive essays often contain references to history and logical conclusions therefrom. But it would be a grave error to suppose that, because he develops so many of his arguments from these sources, his adherence to the Catholic Faith depended solely, or even principally upon them. The supernatural and the mysteries of the supernatural were part and parcel of his faith. It was because he had such firm belief in the Church's teaching that he felt the urge to explain to others the authenticity and infallibility of its authority. Though such a fighter and so confident in the justice of any cause that he supported, he displayed, even in the ordinary affairs of everyday life, extraordinary humility, never assuming knowledge he did not possess or attempting to force his opinions upon those who disagreed with him. He would state his case trenchantly and ruthlessly puncture the arguments of his opponents, but provided a man were honest in the theories he held, he would respect his right to hold them and only attack what he considered to be their falsity. In the controversy he had with Wells over the latter's *Outline of History*, both of them argued fiercely and hit hard, but Belloc was really distressed at Wells's coolness towards him after the fight was over. He had been attacking a thesis that he was convinced was false in the interests of what he believed to be the truth. He had not been disputing Wells's right to hold an opposite opinion, and had no feeling of personal superiority over his opponent.

This humility in matters which he did not feel himself justified in judging or competent to judge was particularly noticeable in his reactions to religion. He might, and frequently did, criticize the policy of leaders of the Church in mundane affairs, but for the priestly office and the religious teaching of the Church he had the deepest respect and never contested that authority. This attitude was entirely consistent with all that he has written and the arguments he has used. He was satisfied that he had found the authoritative witness to Divine truth and he was content to be guided by it, knowing full well the fallibility of merely human opinions and human emotions. In several of his essays he has given glimpses of the satisfaction he experienced from the deeper relations of the spirit with its Creator, and, as in 'The Child is

Born', his feeling of security and peace under the sheltering roof of the Faith.

But it was not in studies on the spiritual life that his great service to the Church consisted. His powerful influence upon English Catholics of his day—and indeed Catholics all over the world—and upon the position of the Church in this country derived from quite a different source.

When Belloc began to make his name as a writer Catholics in England were still under a cloud. Overt persecution, which in the centuries following the Reformation had reduced them to a small despised minority with little or no rights in the country of their birth, had ceased in 1829 when the Act of Emancipation became law, but they were still regarded by the general public as an anti-national clique and hence made to feel the inferiority of their position as compared with the rest of the population. Though entry into the professions had been granted to them by degrees, all the highest offices of the State were still out of their reach. Prolonged propaganda had done its work: the mind of the English had been poisoned against the Faith of their fathers. Into this group of rather timid Catholics Belloc strode with the supreme confidence of youth and unfaltering conviction. So far from apologizing for the Faith that he held and remaining on the defensive, he went straight to the attack denouncing those who through greed had organized the change of religion and pouring scorn on the historians who had shaped history to conceal the plunder. He proceeded, as we have seen, to demonstrate how the Catholic Church had made the civilization of Europe and how England, by an accident as disreputable as it was calamitous, had broken away from the life-springs of her destiny. The effect upon English Catholics of this turning of the tables against those who had oppressed them was profound. They were filled with a new confidence and began to develop a new outlook. Not only did they realize more fully than before the extent and magnificence of their heritage, but they were helped to relate all their pious observances and private devotions to the overriding claims and promises of the Faith. Hope sprang up anew as they felt themselves to be the heirs of the true English tradition relying upon supernatural guidance and the universality of its message. Like one of the ancient prophets

Belloc appeared, with all the personal equipment most needed for the situation, at a moment of hesitation and timidity. Great leaders there had been and were, but the rank and file of Catholics were oppressed by a sense of inferiority. In was his great achievement to sweep all that away and give to history a new meaning. A man of the world, with high talents and influential friends, most of whom knew little or nothing of the Catholic Church, he set himself to explain and magnify the Faith that was in him in all kinds of company, for it was by no means only in his writings that he carried the standard of the Faith into battle. He habitually spoke of it, as he would speak of—say—the law of gravity, as something established and certain, which only ignorance would gainsay, and moreover something which it was as natural to discuss in ordinary conversation as the boat race or a General Election.

Naturally enough there were those among his fellow Catholics who thought this onslaught exaggerated and perhaps dangerous. They had become accustomed to defer in non-religious matters and even in some of their own tentative proposals for a greater measure of justice to Catholics, to the opinions of non-Catholics, and were afraid that Belloc's outspoken challenges would lead to additional restraints. With this kind of person he had little patience, and perhaps it was partly for this reason that he always expressed horror at the possibility of becoming 'an official Catholic'. He had taken a line of his own and was determined not to be identified with any group, however influential, and especially, a group with which he had many points of disagreement. This repugnance to any sort of officialdom may sometimes have caused him to over-emphasize the isolation of his own position and given him a secret pleasure in shocking those whom he felt to be following too passive a line. It also no doubt added to his reluctance to accept any official honour. When asked to accept the award of Companion of Honour he begged to be excused, and he declined to stand for the Professorship of Poetry at Oxford, though this was probably due more to a lasting grudge against the University for having refused him a Fellowship than to the nature of the offer. Also, when without previous intimation, he was informed that he had been granted a Papal honour, his reaction was more one of annoyance than of pleasure. There was, however, one exception to his aversion to these symbols

74

of recognition: he prized his 'bouton' of the Légion d'Honneur and, later, his promotion to be Chevalier of that Order. That may have been partly because he had a higher opinion of French awards than those granted in England: but probably also because acceptance of a French honour did not put him under any obligation to an authority which he had so often attacked.

But though he thus kept ready to his hand, and had no hesitation in using when he thought fit, weapons with which to attack those who would curb his energetic championship of the Faith in England, his lasting work in this domain was constructive. He inspired his fellow Catholics with the broad outlines of their religion, presented to them with a zest and conviction that both instructed them and fired them with a new zeal. The success of his efforts in this campaign may be seen, not only in the greater influence of Catholics in public affairs today than at the time when he began to write, but also in the predominant attitude of Catholic authors of the present time towards Catholicism. No longer does it appear to them so necessary to emphasize the part the Church has played in history. Belloc has established that general thesis, and the writers who continue along these lines are filling in omissions and correcting blemishes rather than vying with him in putting the Church on the map. But there is another noticeable development, particularly among novelists. The tendency now is to take for granted the presence of Catholics in every rank of society and knowledge of the general nature of the dogmas to which they subscribe. The main interest, where Catholic characters appear in novels, seems to be the particular problems that beset them, their weaknesses, and the clash of loyalties in which they are involved. It is the finesses of the Catholic conscience itself, rarely the more obvious differences between the Catholic and non-Catholic outlook on life, that are worked out in the story. This is a change that could hardly have come about in England, had it not been for Belloc's ground work. In France, and other countries in which understanding of the Catholic Church has always been present, this type of novel has long been in existence, but here it is only a recent growth.

But his influence among his fellow Catholics is too well known to need underlining. The countless letters he received during his active lifetime, and those which have poured in to Eleanor and myself since his death, and indeed in those fallow years of his old age when contemplation replaced activity, register in an extraordinary degree the effect upon others of his Catholic writings. Over and over again there have been instances in which correspondents, who have never seen or known him, would express their profound thanks to him, not merely as a writer, but as a man (so direct was the appeal of the words he used), for the encouragement he had given them in their Faith and the light that he had shed upon it. They felt that he was an ally upon whom they could rely, and one who raised them above the difficulties and doubts that beset them into the splendour of the heritage that was theirs.

7   *Controversy*

I THINK it is true to say that Belloc enjoyed controversy while he was engaged in it. But this statement requires qualification. It will be found on examination of his controversial writings that nearly all of them are concerned with defence of the Catholic Church and its claims. He felt it his duty to search out assertions which explicitly or implicitly attacked or misinterpreted some dogma of the Faith he held and to rebut them by argument. But, as he grew older and looked back on a number of such campaigns, he began to desire to be free of them. The very volume and reiteration of the opinions ranged against him produced an atmosphere around him which, though time and again he dissipated it by powerful gusts of reasoning and historical evidence, yet weighed upon him and made him apprehensive, not that he would falter in the Faith that moulded his whole being, but that his peace of mind might become blurred by constant association with minds so inimical to his own. That in fact he continued to the end of his active life in such bouts of controversy must therefore be put down to a sense of duty rather than to inclination; yet, once committed to the fray, his old ardour would return.

He enjoyed the fight because he had supreme confidence in the truth of the causes he defended and in the falsity of those he attacked. Nor did he doubt for a moment his own ability, backed up by truth, to demolish his opponent in argument. That was not conceit (I have said before that there was no conceit in his make-up), for he never undertook a dispute over matters with which he was not conversant or about which he held no strong views. He never exercised his powers to make the worse cause appear the better. In fact desultory arguments carried on by the uninformed reduced him to a state of profound boredom. Time and again, when that sort of argument arose amongst his friends, I have known him cut it short by a sudden change in the conversation or by some such remark as that theological arguments are the result of drinking port. No, when he plunged into a controversy it was with a definite object in view which he thought vital.

Sometimes the occasion would arise from an attack delivered against some statement he had made or some view that he held. His exchanges with Coulton and Dean Inge were usually of that sort. Sometimes he would take the initiative, when he came across a book or an article to which he took strong exception. The standard example of this was his prolonged controversy with Wells over the latter's *Outline of History*. Occasionally, too, he would take part in a platform disputation that had been organized as a sort of gladiatorial show for the benefit of an audience, but he was not attracted by that kind of battle of wits, and produced few of his heavy guns at such entertainments. When acting as chairman to the Shaw-Chesterton debate on 'Do We Agree?', he finished his brief introductory remarks by saying: 'They are about to debate. You are about to listen. I am about to sneer.' And in all probability the thrusts and counter-thrusts that followed, which de-lighted a packed house of listeners, were for him little more than a rather wearisome display of mental gymnastics. When he himself was persuaded later on to hold a public debate with Shaw about what the future holds for us, he broke all the rules of the fencing match in which he was expected to take part, and, almost totally ignoring Shaw's playful thrusts at him, contented himself with pronouncing an eloquent commentary on death (which he reminded his audience was the only thing in the future they could be certain of) enlivened with some admirable stories of his own invention.

The reason for this attitude of Belloc's is pretty clear. Public debates of this kind were not controversy in any real sense. They were sham fights between two prominent literary figures staged with a view to delighting their admirers. For the real fighter, bearing the scars of battles fought for a cause, they were poor stuff. Such sparring, he felt, should be spontaneous and conducted in congenial company where any sort of extravagance was admissible and wit was a by-product rather than a calculated ingredient.

But with controversy proper it was quite different. There the issue was both important and strictly defined. The aim was victory in a contest of reason, so that the plan of campaign had to be prepared and

78

weapons examined. Belloc's strategy in all major contests of this kind was planned on similar lines. He would first explain his object very clearly. He would then give a detailed account of his opponent, introducing first all the qualities in him that he considered admirable and, after that, the shortcomings which vitiated those talents. Next, he would describe exactly what it was in his opponent's thesis that he proposed to attack; and, finally, he would deliver his attack with constant reference to his opponent's words and usually with an abundance of similes to clarify the points he was making. Thus, whenever he crossed swords with Dean Inge he would invariably insist on the Dean's high culture, scholarship, and fluent pen, before pointing out that his *bête noir* was the Catholic Church, and that his insensate antipathy to it led him to abandon the accurate judgement he displayed in other matters. Of Coulton, too, he lists a number of excellences: verbal accuracy, profound erudition, the habit of minutely examining his opponent's terms, lucidity of expression, and a tenacious memory. A catalogue of his defects as an historian follows. First comes a lack of proportion. In this connexion Belloc cites his habit of fixing upon an isolated exception to a whole stream of traditional documentary evidence, and basing his conclusions on that alone; next there is his tendency to explain nearly all the phenomena with which he deals by a single cause, i.e. the malice and ignorance of the Catholic Church. This, in Belloc's view, naturally destroyed his historical judgement and turned him into an advocate. He was ready to accept the most doubtful statements and secondary authority in support of his views, while neglecting the evidence that contradicted them. On the subject of this accusation of advocacy, which, as I have said in an earlier chapter, has been levelled against Belloc himself, it is interesting to note what he says about it.

There is nothing shameful [he writes in *The Case of Dr Coulton*] about advocacy—so long as it is open advocacy. Advocacy is the life and motive of a great profession, and is inseparable from much the most of human intellectual activity; what is more, hardly any man who feels strongly can quite avoid it, even when he is doing his utmost to be impartial. But the vice of permanent advocacy in *history* is fatal. In advocacy we emphasize all that is to be said on

79

our side. We minimize or omit all that is to be said on the other. 'I do not see,' says the advocate, 'why I should provide my opponent with such-and-such a point in his favour. It is for him to discover it.' True; but then the advocacy must be admitted, and must pre-suppose (as we do in our Courts of Law) similar advocacy for the opposing cause. . . . Now the historian is essentially a judge. He is there not to argue a brief, but to find out the truth. That is what Dr Coulton can never understand.

That account of advocacy and the condemnation of it when used in arguing an historical thesis will be generally admitted, but the question may be asked whether Belloc, when attributing so much importance to the Catholic Church in European history, was not guilty of the same fault for which he blamed Coulton when he said that the latter's judgement was vitiated by his anti-Catholic bias. The answer to that question becomes clear from an examination of their respective meth-ods. Whereas Belloc, in the first place, openly states his belief that European civilization derives from the Catholic Church, and, secondly, gives chapter and verse for so believing, Coulton never specifically admits that one of his principal aims is to minimize the Church's influence and point out its shortcomings, and therefore finds it unneces-sary to substantiate the charges he makes by a thorough examination of the whole evidence. That difference between the two men is funda-mental. The reader may take sides with the one or with the other, but all must admit that Belloc parades all his goods in the shop window, whereas Coulton invites inspection of only a single specimen at a time, carefully selected out of his large stock of accumulated facts. If then, Belloc did have recourse to advocacy, his opponents ought to have had no difficulty in proving their charge against him, but there is no in-stance in which they were able to do so. In fact the tables were invari-ably turned against them. They found themselves on the defensive in this as in so many other points of contention.

For Belloc was essentially an attacker. When he did pause to defend himself against charges made by the other side, that was always done in such a way that, so far from losing ground, he contrived at the end of his defence to be nearer to his object than he was before it began.

In his controversy with Wells over the latter's *Outline of History*, he uses a whole armoury of weapons with most damaging effect. It began with a long review of the book in the *London Mercury* followed up by a series of articles in the Catholic Press to which Wells responded with a pamphlet entitled *Mr Belloc Objects*; it was continued by a counter pamphlet by Belloc, *Mr Belloc Still Objects*, and was finished by a full-scale book of some 70,000 words, compiled from his articles, and published in a format similar to that of the *Outline*, which he called *A Companion to Mr Wells's Outline of History*.

Wells perhaps lacked the equability of temperament that makes a good controversialist. His *amour propre* was easily offended, and in his restiveness under criticism he was apt to resort to vituperation rather than argument. Belloc made full use of this weakness, and plied Wells's methods of writing history with epithets that were calculated to sting. But, when challenged, he explained the exact meaning of the words he had used and, by giving examples from the text of Wells's book, left it to his readers to decide whether or not he had used the words justifiably. In one respect his task was made comparatively easy. Wells, with all his talents, was not a scholar, even in his knowledge of science, on which he prided himself, and certainly not in history, in the main lines of which he was the mouth-piece of others. He had little or no acquaintance with original sources. Nevertheless he was no mean opponent, and had on his side his immense popularity as a writer.

As usual, Belloc begins (in his *Companion to Mr Wells's Outline of History*, which gathered together all the previous criticisms he had made and his answers to Wells's defence) by stating his precise reasons for entering upon the controversy. He addresses himself to his fellow Catholics and gives his reasons for so doing: first, because

the issue in such matters lies between the Catholic Church and its modern opponents . . . and soon, with the increasing effect of the Church upon the one hand, the increasing abandonment (outside her boundaries) of all transcendental belief on the other, there will be but two approved camps: the Faith, and its enemies.

Secondly, because

Catholics into whose hands a work of this kind falls . . . may be disturbed in their faith by popular literature of this kind. For the sake of this very small number of chance Catholics, who may suffer from a popular (though ephemeral) work of this kind, I desire to examine the book and distinguish its merits from its absurdities.

Having stated his object, Belloc proceeds, as is his wont in controversy, to enumerate, first, the talents, and, secondly, the short-comings of the man whose work he is attacking. Of the former he ascribes to Wells five, all of great value in one who writes history. These are: clarity of expression and economy in the use of words; a sense of time ('he does see *time* in right scale'); 'a strong power of making the image he has framed in his own mind arise in the mind of his reader'; accuracy in his use of reference books, dates, names, etc.; and, most important of all, sincerity. Wells's defects he summarizes under two main headings: provincialism and rabid reaction against tradition. He explains exactly what he means by these two charges:

> Provincialism [he writes] means a satisfied ignorance: a simple faith in the non-existence of what one has not experienced. Provincialism involves a contempt for anything foreign and, what is worse, an actual denial of things which the provincial person has not been made familiar with.

Of Wells's hatred of anything traditional he writes: 'He suffers these reactions against the Gentry—especially the Gentry of his own country—against soldiers, great military characters in history, against certain contemporaries of his, but, most of all, against the Catholic Church,' and he goes on to show how fatal this hatred is, when it becomes un-reasoning, in anyone setting out to write history.

The main body of Belloc's argument (though he leads his readers through every page of the *Outline*, praising parts of it and exposing the falsity of others) is concerned with two points: the Darwinian theory of Natural Selection and the role of the Catholic Church in history. Against the thesis of the former that blind chance slowly evolves new types through the survival of the fittest, he sets down in great detail and with numerous examples four *a priori* arguments, all of them pro-pounded by scientists since Darwin's time, each of which shows the theory to be mathematically impossible. He follows this with three further arguments from evidence. In these he demonstrates that both human experience and geological record are entirely in favour of fixed types of living beings, but 'if fixed types exist they cannot be due to Natural Selection, for Natural Selection and Fixed Types are contradictory terms'. His example of this is both graphic and amusing:

> If Natural Selection be true, then what we call a pig is but a fleeting vision; all the past he has been becoming a pig; and all the future he will spend evolving out of pigdom, and pig is but a moment's phase in the eternal flux, while, all around us should be quarter-pigs, half-pigs, near-pigs, all-but-pigs, slightly-superior pigs, just beginning—and so on. But there aren't. There are just pigs.

But Wells in his *Outline of History* takes Natural Selection for granted and, in so doing, believes that he is disposing of the idea of a Creator and of design in creation. Moreover he is incensed, as his reply shows, that he, a student of science, should be corrected and accused of propagating scientific theories long ago disproved, by a man who had no special training in the subject at all. This leads him to assert himself and ridicule the objections to those theories, which he seems to have thought Belloc had invented. This in any case would have been unwise, for the objections are themselves unanswerable, nor was Belloc a man to put forward an argument that he was not prepared to support with a volume of evidence; but the fact of course was that all the damning criticisms of Natural Selection, which Belloc set out so convincingly, had, as he had stated, been brought forward by a great number of world-famous scientists years before. Wells was apparently unaware of this, and recklessly challenged Belloc to produce their names, openly stating that he was buttressing his statements with the authority of non-existent experts.

This was an absolutely fatal mistake and one which it is astonishing Wells should have allowed himself to make. So far as this part of the argument went, there was little more that could be said. Belloc at once produced his authorities—some forty of them—with quotations from their works and documentation of the high places all of them held in scientific scholarship. He adds: 'It [the list of names] could, of course, be extended indefinitely by anyone setting out to make a complete total of the first-class scholars who have left Darwinism the wreck it is today.'

So far as I know, Wells never responded to this bombardment: Belloc was left in possession of the field.

The rest of Belloc's *Companion to the Outline of History*—indeed the whole book, for the exposure of Natural Selection was itself the breaking up of an attack upon the Catholic Faith—is concerned with Wells's attempt to ridicule and disprove by history the whole Christian thesis. Never for a moment does he dispute Wells's right to hold the views he did hold about religion; what he criticizes throughout and in great detail is his ignorance of the thing he is attacking and the muddle-headedness of his attack. He follows him relentlessly through all his arguments on the existence of God, the Fall of Man, the nature of religion, the Incarnation, the origins of the Church, and continues right up to the Reformation and its results. To all this destructive criticism Wells makes no reply in his pamphlet. This is how Belloc sums up the position:

> One challenge after another—I know not how many in all, but certainly dozens on dozens—was put down by me clearly and, I hope, methodically throughout a series of articles originally twenty-eight in number, and of such volume that they still will form when rearranged a book not less than 70,000 or 80,000 words. Of all this great mass of destructive criticism which leaves his *Outline* limp and deflated, Mr Wells knows nothing. He leaves it unanswered because he cannot answer it.

In this particular controversy, then, Belloc scores a complete victory. His opponent, after failure in his defence of one position, declines battle and leaves the field.

It would be interesting to know how a similar attack from Belloc's pen, delivered against Gibbon's falsification of history regarding the Church, would have been met. Though this can hardly be called controversy, seeing that there could be no reply from the man who was attacked, yet, as an example of Belloc's controversial methods, it is of considerable importance.

Once again the challenge is presented in a series of articles, each of which is concerned with a particular episode in *The Decline and Fall of the Roman Empire*. Once again we see Belloc carefully defining his target and enumerating the various qualities and defects of the man he is attacking. Once again it is the Catholic Church that he is defending. In these articles, however, there is a fuller documentation of the authorities on which he relies than Belloc is accustomed to provide for his readers. There is, too, a great deal of industrious research.

In a sense these articles are directed against falsifications, omissions, and ignorance of original sources similar to those found in Wells's *Outline of History*, but whereas Wells was admittedly relying upon various living historians for his story of the world, Gibbon has achieved a unique reputation as the historian of a certain period—the period that covers the years in which a Catholic Europe was growing out of the pagan Roman Empire. What therefore might be excused in Wells can by no means be excused in Gibbon. Yet by the time Belloc has finished with him a very formidable list of his mis-statements and suppressions of evidence has been established.

It would be beyond the scope of this chapter to follow Belloc's reasoning in all the particular points dealt with in these articles, but a summary of his arguments in *one* of them will help to show the methods he adopts and the extent of his documentation of the evidence.

In a preliminary essay which he calls 'A Preface to Gibbon' he sets down two general charges and emphasizes the importance he attaches to them.

> In point after point Gibbon, while pretending to rely upon first hand authority, is really relying upon secondary authorities belonging to the generation immediately before his own. In point after point he either knows nothing of the original evidence (and therefore comes to a demonstrably false conclusion), or knows it only through the writings of others who have already garbled it. It is high time this feature in the chief of the anti-Catholic historians who have written in the English tongue was exposed. . . . No better task can be conceived than the production of . . . a good essay, well documented by a Catholic scholar, and this followed by a critical edition

85

with notes exposing the errors, suppositions and misrepresentations which mark the whole of this voluminous and entertaining attack upon the Church.

He then proceeds, in the articles that follow, to give specimens himself of the kind of detailed criticism that he urges Catholic scholars to undertake.

One of these specimens is concerned with Gibbon's remarks about a sect known as the Ebionites. It will serve as an example of the thoroughness of Belloc's refutation of Gibbon's theses.

According to Gibbon the Ebionites constituted the original Church. They were Jews and they denied the Divinity of Christ, a dogma which he claims only arose later on when pagans (who were familiar with the idea of the divine in human form) came into the Church. These new Gentile churches began to preach this novelty but the original Jewish Church (i.e. the Ebionites) never accepted it. There was no such person as Ebion, the supposed founder of the sect, but the name merely meant 'poor men', and was applied to them because after the destruction of Jerusalem, they removed to Pella and lived there in great poverty.

That is Gibbon's description of the origins of the Church, according to which the doctrine of the Divinity of Christ (the central point of the Church's teaching) was imposed upon a society which originally had no idea of it.

Belloc's refutation of this theory is exhaustive in its thoroughness. No one could complain in this instance that he fails to give his authorities for each statement that he makes. In fact it is his research, fully recorded, which shows the insufficiency of Gibbon's reading and explodes his theory.

First, he puts forward two negative arguments: that there is no protest to be found in any other Church against the denial or ignoring of the Incarnation by the early Jewish Church at Jerusalem, as there certainly would have been among the Gentile converts had such a denial existed; and that the violent hostility of the non-Christian Jews to the new Faith arose precisely from the latter's claim to the Divinity of Christ. As positive evidence he cites in particular St Ignatius, Hegessipus, and St Justin, all of whom lived in the first century and a half after the Christian era. He quotes St Ignatius, the earliest of the three, who was a boy at the time of Pentecost, to the effect that the doctrine of the Incarnation is the original doctrine of the Church, and that some movement had begun in his time which tended to whittle down this original affirmation of Christ's Divinity. From Hegessipus, who was himself a Jew and had visited all the main early Churches, we learn that he found no divergence of opinion at Jerusalem on the doctrine of the Incarnation until one named Thebutis, after the death of James the first bishop, started a heresy denying the Divinity of Christ and allying itself with the Jewish feeling against the idea of divinity in a man. The third witness, St Jerome, also a Jew and well acquainted with the Church of Jerusalem, states that the only real test of orthodoxy is whether a man accepts the full doctrine in the matter of Christ, and goes on to emphasize the Incarnation as a chief part of that doctrine.

In the same convincing way Belloc arrays his evidence against Gibbon's claim that there was no such man as Ebion, but that the Ebionites were the poverty-stricken remnants of the original Church, which knew nothing of Christ's Divinity. This claim is essential to Gibbon's theory, for if an heresiarch, Ebion, existed, then 'Ebionites' could not have been a name given to the original Church. Belloc quotes at length seven witnesses, including Origen on whom Gibbon had relied for his theory. From these witnesses he proves three things: that the Ebionites were regarded by all of them as heretics; that their founder was a man named Ebion; and that the chance that the name Ebion meant 'poor man' was used by several of these witnesses to point the moral of the 'poverty' of his doctrine, but all who made this play upon words recognized that Ebion was a man, the founder of the heresy. The crowning success of Belloc's research was to have discovered the passage in Origen (unnoticed by Gibbon and his followers) in which he mentions the man Ebion.

I have gone at some length into this particular controversy (though, even so, I have compressed into a page or two what Belloc deals with at length, with full quotations of his supporting evidence and the dates and environment of his witnesses), because it provides a good example of his powers of research and detailed documentation. He has often (and not unjustly) been accused of making statements in his historical work with no reference to authorities. He has more than once given his reasons for this practice, holding that an historian's business is to give a true picture of the past without interrupting the sequence of events by a host of documentary notes which nine-tenths of his readers will not take the trouble to verify. He has also demonstrated more than once that the references historians have made to authorities have sometimes on inspection been found to have little or no bearing upon the point under discussion.

Whether or not Belloc is justified in his repugnance to the insertion of such notes in his history, it becomes perfectly clear from the essays in controversy we have been considering that in this department of writing he is prepared to substantiate every statement he makes and every argument he uses by reference to the sources from which they spring. His forceful and sometimes ruthless attitude towards his opponents has led casual observers to see him merely as a domineering personality bent upon the discomfiture of those with whom he is disputing. Such a view is only partially true. He does indeed pour scorn upon ignorance masquerading as learning, and is well equipped with satire as well as hard blows to counter wilful distortion of facts. But neither his entry into controversy nor the use he makes of the weapons at his disposal is prompted by a desire to score a personal success over a rival. He intends to win the battle, but it is the victory of a cause that he has at heart. Every now and then he allows his ardent faith to break through his clear-cut reasoning and gives a hint of the profound feeling that inspires him. There can be few finer sentences in the whole literature of controversy than the monosyllabic rhetoric with which he sums up a dispute with Dean Inge: 'Our dead are with us, and the Mother of God is ours.'

8 *A Note on Belloc's Verse*

To write of Belloc without mentioning his verse would be to leave out that part of his work which he himself valued most highly. In conversation he would treat his immense contribution to prose literature in an offhand way. Sometimes on re-reading a passage he would pronounce it good, but very often (though the principles that informed his writing never changed) he would dismiss it as a mere means of making a living. With his verse it was different. I have never heard him disparage it. Indeed, for the gifts of the Muse, whether to himself or to others, he had a deep respect almost amounting to reverence. In his *Milton* he wrote:

> How towering verse comes to be written by mortals none have explained nor can, save by inspiration; which is as much as to say that something divine is revealed in the poetic speech, not through the poet's will but through some superior will using the poet for its purpose. It is the afflatus of the God.

It is perhaps owing to this attitude of Belloc's towards verse that his total output is comparatively small. His strong sense of the majesty and music of words, their order and appropriateness to their subject, and the picture produced by them of the vision in his mind—all this made for prolonged experiment and assiduous polishing. It was often years before a poem was completed to his satisfaction. I have, for example, before me as I write a sheet of paper on which are written, in a handwriting often difficult to decipher and with numerous erasions and insertions, the first drafts of his poem 'Tarantella'. The framework of the poem as it eventually appeared is there—the refrain

> Do you remember an Inn, Miranda,
> Do you remember an Inn?

and the sudden change of tempo in the final lines beginning,

> Nevermore, Miranda,
> Nevermore.

For the rest, there are jotted down tentative versions of some of the jingling lines that characterize the dance music of the poem. For example:

> And the jeers and the cheers of the young muleteers
> Who had not got a penny and who wouldn't pay to any

or:

> And the swirl and the twirl of the girl
> In her stedding and the hay that was a bedding

but these are no more than fragments, still unpolished, suggesting the general music of the piece, and not as yet shaped and fitted into its structure. Quite a number of the lines that eventually found a place in the poem are not there at all. For instance,

> And the fleas that tease in the High Pyrenees

and all the sonorous lines that follow

> Nevermore, Miranda,
> Nevermore.

Instead of the lines that complete the poem in its final form there are phrases and half phrases jotted down, such as:

> No more dancing, no more
> song,
> No more all night long

which appear to be reminders of the changed rhythm rather than serious attempts to find the perfect words with which to clothe it.

This sheet is typical of hundreds of others that have been preserved, from illegible scribbles on scraps of paper to carefully written stanzas approximating to the form in which they eventually appeared in his published collections of verse. An examination of them, especially when combined with memories of the way Belloc would break into a conversation with snatches of verse he had just composed or which had suddenly formed themselves in his mind, gives some idea not only of the processes of his craftsmanship but also of the extent to which the vision and language of poetry were an ever present background to his thoughts. Undoubtedly he possessed an unusual facility for the composition of rhyming verse, but with this facility was combined a strong critical sense which forbade him, on the one hand, to distort, for the sake of the rhythm, the smooth—it would seem inevitable—run of words appropriate to the particular image he was engaged in evoking, and on the other, to depart in the slightest degree from the intensely personal outlook with which he regarded the majesty, the pathos, and the incongruities of life. Often among these sheets of jottings the word 'bad' in brackets is to be found after some experimental line, and usually, on inspection, one can detect in the condemned words something foreign to the character of the piece in which they occur, or else something subtly out of tune with Bellocian ways of thought or modes of expression. They might have suited another writer: they did not suit Belloc. In this connexion it is interesting that he always seemed dissatisfied with that stanza in the Dedicatory Ode that has proved so popular and been so often quoted:

> From quiet homes and first beginning,
> > Out to the undiscovered ends,
> There's nothing worth the wear of winning,
> > But laughter and the love of friends.

For some reason, possibly because it was so often torn from its setting and served up as a kind of maxim, but more probably because he felt that the sentiment it contained was slightly out of place in the particular poem in which it occurred, he viewed the lines with mild disfavour and was obviously bored when admirers quoted them to him.

Quite a large proportion of his verse is made to amuse. Besides the separate publications, such as the two *Books of Beasts*, the *Cautionary Tales*, *The Modern Traveller*, *More Peers*, and *Ladies and Gentlemen*, there are numerous pieces—epigrams, ballades, songs, etc.—which have infected readers of all sorts with his individual humour. In these verses two points stand out: first, that his technique remains on the high level that characterizes his serious poems, and, secondly, that the humour that has delighted both old and young readers is peculiarly his own—extravaganza mingled with satire, wit, delightful absurdities which nevertheless mirror the foibles of a particular era and various grades of society, and sheer joyous fun with no *arrière pensées*. All these verses must have run readily from his pen, yet the perfection of wording and rhythm cannot have been the result of mere facility. Each of them is a work of art that conceals the critical revision that has been expended upon it.

Others better qualified than I am have commented on Belloc's verse. Those who admire the classic form and those who delight in the melody of song have praised it highly, but those wedded to the rhythms and language of contemporary poetry have shown little appreciation for it. That is natural enough, for the aims and diction of modern poets appear to be in many respects divorced from those of traditional verse. Their object (or perhaps one should say, their compelling urge) is to express *themselves*—their individual reactions to events and scenes—through the medium of a language and rhythms adapted to, or actually invented for, their purpose. A poet of the classic tradition on the other hand acts rather as the recipient—perhaps the interpreter—of a vision that comes from outside himself; and in endeavouring to re-create it he imposes upon himself certain canons of expression. Again in his *Milton* (in which book and in *Avril* is to be found most of what he has written on the structure of verse) Belloc says: 'He [Milton] felt to his marrow the creative force of restraint, proportion, unity—and that is the classic.'

There are then in Belloc's verse-structure two predominant traits: the classic form and the quality of song. The latter characteristic is borne out by the fact that so many of his poems have been set to music, and that for a number of them he himself composed tunes as he wrote them. Those who have heard him sing such poems as 'The Winged Horse' or 'Tarantella' or 'Halnacker Mill' to the tunes he made for them will realize how closely wedded are the words to music.

That his verse is written in classic form hardly needs saying. What is more interesting is to trace the influence of earlier poets on his writing. In spite of his profound admiration for Milton's poetry, I can find little or no echo of Milton's rhythms in Belloc's verse. He did not experiment in blank verse, of which Milton was such a master, and though he has put on record his high esteem for the language and rhythms of such lyrics as 'L'Allegro' and 'Il Penseroso', their music is not his. With Shakespeare it is different. It is not necessary to know that, as a boy in his teens, Belloc lay for hours together on the Downs over-looking Amberley enthralled by Shakespeare's sonnets, in order to recognize in his own sonnets and some of his other poems the rhythms and modes of expression, and even now and then the play upon words, that characterize Shakespeare's. Often the opening line or the first few lines are strikingly Shakespearean, as for example:

> Youth gave you to me, but I'll not believe
> That Youth will, taking his quick self, take you.

or,

> Now shall the certain purpose of my soul
> By blind and empty things controlléd be

or again,

> Believing Truth is staring at the sun
> Which but destroys the power that could perceive.

or the whole of the two sonnets, one of which begins:

> That which is one they shear and make it twain

and the other:

> Because I find foreknowledge in my soul.

In all these, and in others too, I think most readers will recognize some-thing of that poetic atmosphere which Shakespeare created.

In his 'Heroic Poem in Praise of Wine' there are lines and a general lilt which suggests the influence of Dryden. Indeed Belloc must have felt this himself, for I remember, when he had just completed the poem, he was troubled by the thought that in his line,

> And sank to sleep on Ariadne's breast

he might inadvertently have repeated one of Dryden's.

Half French as he was by birth, and even more French in his love and understanding of France, it would be surprising if Belloc's verse had remained unaffected by the poetry of his native country, and no doubt those well acquainted with the cadences and rhythms of the French poets will find echoes of them in it. My own knowledge of French poetry is too fragmentary and superficial for me to offer an opinion of any value, yet one or two of his lyrics, perhaps notably the one beginning,

How shall I round the ending of a story

seem to be reminiscent of the vividness and beauty of Ronsard's verse; and the 'Ballade to Our Lady of Czestochowa' has much of the character, and an almost literal translation of the refrain, of Villon's 'Ballade of Our Lady' which begins

Dame des cieulx, regente terrienne.

But however many comparisons may be made between Belloc's verse and that of his predecessors, he remains one of our most individual poets, and in his comparatively small output he strikes many different notes and stirs many different emotions in the reader. Whether he is writing of glory on the field of battle, or addressing a child with understanding tenderness, or revelling in the sheer beauty of landscape, or pouring biting satire upon injustice or false pretensions; whether his theme is of love, or death, or the promise of immortality; even when he is amusing us with his light-hearted ironical verse and pointed epigrams, or singing extravagant songs—there is always present the genuinely personal touch of one who feels strongly what he writes; always the vigour of the man and the vision of the poet; and always the restrained diction of the classic form.

Who but Belloc could have written, for example, that magnificent sonnet of the phantom revolutionary army which begins

I, from a window where the Meuse is wide

and ends in a sestet of outstanding poetic vision:

And fading still, and pointing to their scars,
    They rose in lessening cloud, where grey and high
Dawn lay along the heaven in misty bars;
    But watching from that eastern casement, I
    Saw the Republic splendid in the sky,
And round her terrible head the morning stars.

Or who could fail to recognize Belloc as the author of the 'Dedication on the Gift of a Book to a Child', a poem which illustrates that rare gift of being able to change from playful jesting to an exquisite serious-ness with a naturalness and poetic sense born of the conviction that all human faculties are created for the glory of God?

> Child, do not throw this book about!
> Refrain from the unholy pleasure
> Of cutting all the pictures out!

and then in the last stanza,

> And when your prayers complete the day,
> Darling, your little tiny hands
> Were also made, I think, to pray
> For men that lose their fairylands.

But every line of verse that Belloc wrote came, sculptured and polished, straight from the heart of his being—from his loves and hates, his laughter and tears, and, above all, from his faith. I have said in an earlier chapter that, while it is rare with him to allow personal feelings to appear in his prose works, his verse is far more self-revealing. This revelation takes many forms. In 'The Fanatic', for example, though it is not himself that he describes so drolly and with such pathos, yet it is a man whose purpose and fate he felt to be closely linked with his own.

> He was a man that could not keep
> His money (when he had the same)
> Because of creditors who came
> And took it from him; and he gave
> So freely that he could not save.
> But all the while a sort of whim
> Persistently remained with him,
> Half admirable, half absurd:
> To keep his word, to keep his word . . .
> By which he did not mean what you
> And I would mean (of payments due
> Or punctual rental of the Flat—
> He was a deal too mad for that)

95

But—as he put it with a fine
Abandon, foolish or divine—
But 'That great word which every man
Gave God before his life began'.

Belloc, too, had forgone much, suffered much through keeping his
word. In another poem his cry is more personal, more poignant,

England, to me that never have malingered,
    Nor spoken falsely, nor your flattery used,
Nor even in my rightful garden lingered:—
    What have you not refused?

'The Death and Last Confession of Wandering Peter' is another imaginative half-picture of himself.

Almighty God will surely cry
    'St Michael! Who is this that stands
With Ireland in his dubious eye,
    And Périgord between his hands,

And on his arm the stirrup thongs,
    And in his gait the narrow seas,
And in his mouth Burgundian songs,
    But in his heart the Pyrenees?'

But that is a thanksgiving rather than a lament.

Then there are the numerous songs of the sea and sailing, of the
countryside and the hills, most of which have in them a strong personal note. And finally there are those that tell of the faith that bore
him up through life, and those of which his wife, whom he loved so
devotedly and mourned so inconsolably, was the inspiration.

There will be no meeting of eyes, nor any blessing
    After the run.
The lips are still, and the hand has ceased from caressing.
    There is nothing more to be done.

But judgement of a poet, in its final analysis, is not concerned so much with the things about which he writes or even with the personality of the man, as with the quality and effect of his verse. Belloc's is like marble carved by the hand of a master into a hundred different shapes, but always retaining the hardness of the material in which he is working. The chiselling is adapted to the work in hand, but the result is always clean-cut and satisfying. To many it is far more than satisfying. It is a joy and an inspiration.

9 *King's Land*

Stand thou forever among human Houses,
House of the Resurrection, House of Birth;
House of the rooted hearts and long carouses,
Stand, and be famous over all the Earth.

ING'S LAND, Belloc's home for nearly half a century, was almost
a part of himself, so perfectly did it fulfil his moods and his
affections. He has written of it in 'A Remaining Christmas':

This house stands low down upon clay near a little river. It is quite
cut off from the towns, no one has built near it. Every cottage for a
mile or more is old, with here and there a modern addition. The
church of the parish (which was lost of course three and a half centuries ago, under Elizabeth) is as old as the Crusades. It is of the
twelfth century. The house of which I speak is in its oldest parts of
the fourteenth century at least, and perhaps earlier, but there are
modern additions. One wing of it was built seventy years ago at the
south end of the house, another at the north end, twenty years ago.
Yet the tradition is so strong that you would not tell from the outside, and hardly from the inside, which part is old and which part is
new. For indeed, the old part itself grew up gradually, and the eleven
gables of the house show up against the sky as though they were of
one age, though in truth they are of every age down along all these
five hundred years and more.

He goes on to describe something of what was to be found inside
the house—the chapel, the dining-room with its open fireplace and
great oak table, and the hall which he himself had built—but the
essential part of this essay is devoted to the traditional Christmas that
was celebrated there, an annual highlight in the life of the house. Of
what King's Land meant to him in its less festive moments over all
those years he has not written, except in one short poem quoted at the

head of this chapter, but he certainly treasured it as a refuge and place of peace—the calm at the centre of the whirlwind of his life.

It was from Slindon, with his wife in a trailer attached to his bicycle, that he came first to Shipley in 1905 seeking a permanent home in Sussex. King's Land, with a cottage and great windmill beside it, stands where a bridle path leaves the lane that passes on towards the church. The house had been the village shop and was then vacant. It fulfilled all his hopes and desires, and from that moment his mind was made up. He bought it together with the mill, the cottage, and the fields beside it, and thenceforward it became the centre of his life. Not that he often passed many consecutive nights there during his active life, for he was always on the move, backwards and forwards to London, lecturing here, there and everywhere up and down the country, constantly crossing the Channel on long or short visits to France or further afield in quest of topographical material for his historical work, sailing the seas in one or other of his boats, visiting friends. Yet every time he returned to Shipley—often exhausted, sometimes ill—he experienced a peace of mind and a sense of permanence that no other place could bring him in like measure. Nor indeed were these sensations peculiar to Belloc. King's Land and Shipley have cast a spell on others too. I myself have felt it strongly, and perhaps I may be allowed to digress for a moment by quoting what I wrote twenty-five years ago of this enchantment, which has remained with me ever since.

There are some places, so it seems to me, which have in them the quality of eternity. They are, as it were, little plots from the garden of Heaven to be re-inclosed when the fitful breeze of time has blown itself out, and the universe is left undisturbed again with God.

One of such places is known to me and there may be others; for I cannot think that one spot alone in the world can be thus singled out for eternity to the exclusion of all others, though, for my part, I know only one. For convenience I will call it Knights-at-Rest, since there are indeed knights at rest in one at least of its quiet fields. For me it is holy ground. And if it be said that this holiness is a figment of my mind and not inherent in the place itself, but induced by long

99

sojourning there and happy associations, I answer that, though I have often visited it, and never unhappily, I have passed no more than a few nights there in all; that the very first evening I saw it there fell upon me a sense of the presence of eternal things; and that at least one other human being, who has even less close associations with it than I have, has known the same sensation and holds it true.

As in the soul that is near to God there exist a wide calm and a silence that pervade the jangling noises of life, so, whenever I come to Knights-at-Rest, I am caught up as onto a mountain top, where even the loudest sounds beat harmlessly upon the protecting silence, and the voices of the village come to my ears muted and full of peace. Nor is this a mere trick of the senses brought on by the experience of a few calm evenings of summer. I have known Knights-at-Rest in all kinds of weather, and, though over other country villages there dwells the contentment of a quiet repose—a sweet remoteness from the rush of life—yet the difference between such places and Knights-at-Rest is for me so marked as to escape comparison. Knights-at-Rest does indeed include all that is most desirable in the villages of England, but it possesses, at least in my eyes and those of my friend, what *they* do not possess, and what I have called the quality of eternity.

But it must not be thought that King's Land was just a place of rest and day-dreams. After a good night's rest Belloc, if he was not writing, would be busy organizing the work of his gardener Frank Laker—a true Sussex type of the old school who to his dying day used to wear a bowler hat on his walks across the fields to and from his work—or superintending the farming of some 150 acres of land that he had bought in the parish. Then there were the frequent visits of his friends with prolonged discussions, songs, and convivial conversation. Sometimes Wilfrid Blunt, whose fine Jacobean house New Buildings was only two or three miles away, would appear driving a tandem of Arab horses and bringing with him guests from his house party. Frequently, too, Belloc and his wife would dine at New Buildings. In a sense King's Land was as alive with movement and incident as was his life elsewhere. But it was a different kind of activity. The pressure of the battle with life, in which he always seemed to be engaged, relaxed, and though he would often dictate to his secretary for hours on end, either in his study or the hut he had built for himself in the garden, and though he was constantly occupied with the responsibilities of country owner-ship and family affairs, he found relief from the stress of London and the fatigue of travel. He guarded his home jealously from such con-tacts, preferring to have no telephone in the house, so that he could not be rung up by publishers and editors and those who would recall him to the outside world. Should some over-bold reporter or other inquisitive person appear at what served as the front door of the house, but is actually a windowed door opening directly into the living-room, he would usually get short shrift. But others, often Americans, who not infrequently turned up with the engaging (though not always convenient) self-introduction that they just wanted to shake Mr Belloc by the hand, were invited in with great courtesy. I remember one such, an American, who arrived as we were having lunch. He was brought into the dining-room and given refreshment. He began at once to tell us how greatly impressed he was by what he had seen of the people of Shipley. It appeared that he had been to one of the inns and discovered that no less than six of the local inmates had swum the English Channel. This piece of news surprised us a good deal till we learnt that, as each told his tale, the kindly American had treated him with free drinks as a token of respect for his achievement.

But as well as hospitality to visitors, work at his books or on the farm, and periods of rest, there were recurrent special occasions. The Christmas that he has himself described was one. New Year's Eve was another. This was made up of a peculiar mixture of tradition and super-stition. Shortly before midnight all the doors of the house (and King's Land boasted eight outside doors) were opened, and just before the stroke of the hour, everyone would go out into the lane and await the chime of the church bells ringing in the New Year. Belloc would then select a small pebble from the path and place it in his pocket. After which, the shivering household would hurry back to a blazing fire in the dining-room and drink each other's healths.

Less exacting, but just as carefully organized, were the periodical mornings devoted to the bottling of wine. Preparations for these occasions had to be made some weeks in advance. First of all Belloc would go over to France to taste and select his wine, which would be shipped over the Channel in great barrels. Then there was the cleaning and drying of the bottles and the soaking of the corks. At least six people had to be assembled for the bottling itself, and, if possible, a fine sunny day chosen. Frank Laker usually presided, cross-legged at the barrel, and Belloc would be in charge of the bottling machine. Of the rest of the party one would be seated at a small table with a funnel and a few empty bottles, and it was his duty to receive the filled bottles, brought to him from the cellar, and adjust the height of the wine in them so that it reached half-way up the neck. This done, he would pass it to another member of the team to be taken to the bottling machine and have the cork inserted. Two more would be employed in taking the corked bottles and stacking them at the end of the hall. All operations had to be done at speed, for the less time the wine was exposed to the air, the less chance there was of it going sour. It was a tiring but rewarding morning's work.

On such occasions as these Belloc would show characteristics which, though always part of his make-up and liable to appear at unexpected moments, were in marked contrast with his carefree enjoyment of the society of his friends. He was meticulous in his preparations, precise in the way things should be done, and insistent on prompt action—the captain of his ship, yet always ready to relax as soon as the voyage was over.

But the variety of his interests was phenomenal, and he had moods that fitted them all. King's Land provided an atmosphere in which all of them could mature. It was there that so many of his writings had their genesis, writings so diverse that it would be difficult to find any domain of life or thought that he had not explored. For he could write with the biting scorn of a prophet confronted by treachery and deceit, or with the humility of one who knows the fallibility of all human strivings; with the tenderness of a child, or the ferocity of a soldier in battle. He could create beauty seen through the eyes of a lover. He could communicate the exhilaration of those who dare upon the high seas. The flamboyant braggadocio of a Cyrano was his to flaunt, as was the loveliness of the South Country his to enshrine. He could do all

The Windmill (1911)

King's Land, painted by a journeyman artist (1910)

these things because each was a part of him, and King's Land was the hallowed spot in which he could give rein to every side of his nature. There, on the last day of the year, he might be seen in his study balancing his personal accounts to the last penny; but from there have come, over and over again, recklessly generous gifts to all manner of people in need. In that house there were always present visible signs of his inconsolable mourning for his wife, yet from there issued countless letters of consolation and hope to his friends in their bereavements. In the little chapel upstairs and in the Masses so frequently said there resided the guiding principle of all his actions and the source and inspiration of three-quarters of his writing. The rest of the house was alive with his myriad activities, with 'laughter and the love of friends'.

In his later years, when the effects of his illness and the physical infirmity due to old age kept him year in and year out within the house of so many memories, joyous and sad, he would sit for long hours together reading and musing in his study, contented that he should have lived so long and jokingly appealing to his friends to support him in a plan to stretch human life to greater lengths. 'Death', he would say, 'means such a change of habits.' Yet all through his life he was acutely conscious of mortality, and undoubtedly in those years of comparative inaction he contemplated his own passage into eternity and prepared himself for it.

10 *The Last Hours*

THOSE who have strong faith are accustomed to looking death in the face. It was so with Belloc. Mortality was an undercurrent running through all his work. It saddened him that all those he loved and all the things that so delighted him on earth—hills and the sea and the highest achievements of man's craftsmanship—should carry in them the seeds of dissolution and death, but he never deceived himself or acted as if that were not so. His *desiderium* for all that had made life so splendidly worth living was inextricably linked in him with that other emotion which he has so often expressed in the figure of a ship, battered by the wind and high seas, coming at last into the sheltered calm of the harbour. He knew that the battle well fought had its reward in peace, but he did not imagine that the passage from time to eternity, from the known to the unknown, would be as easy as tying his weather-beaten ship to its moorings in port. Death implied an abrupt 'change of habits' and faith alone inspired confidence in the change. Yet when death came to him there was no apprehension, only peace.

From the moment of his accident * he remained unagitated and apparently free from pain. During his journey with Eleanor in an ambulance to the hospital of the Franciscan Missionary Nursing Sisters at Guildford he was fully conscious and discussed with one of the

---

* The accident occurred in his study at King's Land on July 16th, 1953. He had been somewhat restless during the morning, and shortly before lunch Eleanor had taken him a glass of sherry. She returned to the kitchen where she was cooking lunch, and about ten minutes later she smelt burning. She hurried back to the study and found the room full of smoke and her father lying on his back on the hearth rug. Some glowing coals had been scattered on the rug and were burning through his coat. It is impossible to say exactly what had happened. Perhaps he had been poking the fire and had somehow dislodged the coals and had then tripped and fallen on them. Perhaps he had had a slight stroke. Fortunately our son Julian and a friend of his were in the house and helped Eleanor to render first aid. The local nurse was fetched in a few minutes, and the doctor arrived shortly after.

ambulance attendants the war medals he was wearing on his uniform. At the entrance of the hospital he was met by Sister Bernadette who, a few years previously, had nursed him through an illness at King's Land. He recognized her at once, and his smile showed the pleasure he felt in seeing her again. That night he had to be given a deep anaesthetic while the burns on his back were being dressed and bandaged, and the next day, Monday, he was conscious only at intervals. However, he was able to talk a little to Eleanor. All Tuesday he remained unconscious, and Eleanor was with him alone, save for the comings and goings of the devoted Sisters nursing him, in unruffled peace. That evening he received the Last Sacraments. On Wednesday he rallied a little and was able to talk to us and to Lady Phipps who had come to see him. Indeed in the evening he was well enough to drink some wine poured out for him by our son Philip, that we had brought him from King's Land. But late that night Sister Bernadette told us that he was sinking. The next day was the Feast of Our Lady of Carmel, and there were gathered round his bed some of those he loved best—Elizabeth, his younger daughter, Stella, the widow of his youngest son Peter, Edith Rance, who for twenty years had been his faithful housekeeper, John and Mary Morton, Eleanor, myself, and our two sons Philip and Julian. His own son Hilary, who had flown over from California on hearing of his illness, arrived at the hospital a few minutes after his death.

All the morning and through the early afternoon he sat almost erect, propped up by pillows. His eyes remained closed and his whole demeanour was one of majestic reverie, as though already he had turned from the things of earth and was contemplating at last the vision he had so long pursued with the eyes of faith. As the minutes slipped by Elizabeth recited the rosary, in which all joined, and Philip read aloud the beautiful prayers for the dying. From the bed there came no visible sign, only a pervading peace. By degrees his steady breathing became less pronounced, and the pallor of his skin more transparent. But the strength and serenity of his expression remained unchanged. And so, almost imperceptibly, he passed untroubled from the life in which he had loved, and sung, and fought, into one to which he had so long looked forward.

It is fitting that he should have died on a Feast Day of the Queen of Heaven, on whom he had so often called and whom he had so resolutely defended. During his life he had frequently been a Cassandra among the prophets, warning England of the dangers in which she stood and receiving scant attention. But at his death the position was reversed. His fears of dereliction at the end of his life,

> When friend, and fire, and home are lost
> And even children drawn away,

were to be proved groundless, and the recurrent note in the hundreds of letters we received after his death was one of love and friendship. He himself in a letter to Gilbert Chesterton, before the latter was a Catholic, wrote of 'Our Dear Lady, the blessed Mother of God', 'She never fails us. She has never failed me in any demand.' He need have had no fears, who could write of Her in another place

> You shall receive me when the clouds are high
> With evening, and the sheep attain the fold.
> This is the faith that I have held and hold,
> And this is that in which I mean to die.

PART II

REMINISCENCES OF H.B.
by Eleanor Jebb

11 *Chelsea*

Now fades the glimmering landscape on the sight
And all the air a solemn stillness holds.

WHERE do I first remember him? When we moved from 36 Holywell, Oxford, to 104 Cheyne Walk, Chelsea, in 1900. There were two of us: Louis, my brother, and myself. Elizabeth, Hilary, and Peter, the other three, were to be born at 104.

In 1900 H.B. was in his thirtieth year, so that his energy and vigour seemed on a gigantic scale in those few, fitful, vivid memories of his invasion into our nursery world or our supervised meetings with him downstairs in the little house which my mother loved so well and all about which lie my first memories.

His study lay to the left of the front door in the narrow little hall; the window looked out upon the Thames Embankment across a tiny patch of railed-in garden in which there seemed to flourish a profusion of chickweed. I used to ponder about this and wonder why he did not climb out of his window and collect it, because it flourished beyond the reach of our tiny arms through the railings.

The dining-room was long and low and lay on the right of the front passage; it contained the same table we have in King's Land dining-room. This table is old and long and made of oak; it was once a sideboard in an Oxford college. Mamma and Papa found it in a shop and bought it for £10 when they were married and first settled in Oxford at 36 Holywell. My father would sometimes lift us up in the dining-room until our heads gently touched the ceiling—to us a curiously ecstatic novelty! There came a day when, three years old and returning from a holiday, I found by standing on tiptoe I could just see level with this wonderful table-top and there stretched away before my infant eyes a seemingly limitless dark glassy lake which astonished me. Before I had only known the marvel of its legs, massive and carved, and the great tent-like covering of its solid top.

My father treasured this table. To his perpetual joy Edie Rance, our housekeeper, kept it in most beautiful condition, and after she left us in 1934 no one ever had the like of her touch and power to keep its gleaming surface the same. Wine marks, soup stains, candle-grease, all disappeared like magic under her deft hands and knowledge of its needs.

Frances and Gilbert Chesterton lived at Battersea at this time and used to come over the bridge to see us frequently. Frances had a deep tenderness of heart for children and a great understanding of them. She gave me the first carnation I had ever seen—it was in her buttonhole—and I carry the undimmed magic of its scent and beauty to this day. It had to be left for the night when I was put to bed—but I only parted from it having seen it safely in a cup of water and put into the doll's house. Oddly enough, I have no memories in those Chelsea days of H.B. and Gilbert together, but Gilbert is a vivid memory making his puppets come to life for us in the nursery, sitting perilously on a chair far too small for his vast form and rumbling out romances and feuds, at which he laughed almost more than we did.

Beyond our large nursery windows lay the glistening Thames, with the ceaseless entertainment of all that commercial river life; sailing barges with brown sails, little tugs, puffing up and down and lowering their funnels at the bridges, and the gliding crying gulls swooping and soaring—never a dull moment.

The day that Elizabeth and I threw out some old toys from the night nursery back window on to Robinson's shed roof was a black and fearful day because we tasted for the first time the roar of Papa's wrath. Nannie had reported this misdoing to H.B. There lay the toys in tragic disarray—a small shabby monkey, some kind of mechanical toy and some of those inevitable playtime wooden bricks. We had been warned before about wanton behaviour of this sort. Parts of Robinson's roof had glass skylights, and these of course we were hoping to smash holes in! He stood there before the window with us—his hands behind his back, enormous and powerful: 'This must never, never happen again.—How dare you?' Tones of thunder—and it never did happen again. But in spite of that lesson years later we tossed our bonnets over the King's Land windmill in youthful disobedience of his just commands.

In the winter of 1904 near Christmas-time H.B. was lost in a fog one night and caught cold which became pneumonia. I remember the hush in the house and Mamma's silent anxiety. Dr Penny thought that he might die, so H.B. was anointed and given the last sacraments by Father Hayes. H.B. was always very proud of this episode and often talked about it. When he began slowly to recover I was carried in by Nannie Drewitt to see him and was very taken aback by the curiously red beard which had grown on his chin. I remember his weakness as being so unfamiliar. He gave me a wonderful smile, opening his eyes, which softened for me the effect of the beard. There was a latent eagerness about him which must have been his restless soul beginning to resent the captivity of bed. When I saw him smile at Frances Phipps on his deathbed I remembered the smile of the far-off Chelsea days.

If we saw him arrive in a hansom at 104 he used seemingly to leap from it in an astonishingly agile bound—all one parabola! The heavy sloping doors would fly open, he was on the pavement in a flash and his familiar resonant voice could be heard in the little hall below. How thin he was in those days! Sometimes he carried a straw boater, and always lots of newspapers.

There was a telephone in the hall, a curious little instrument screwed to the wall, which my father had installed immediately upon taking over the tenancy of the house. But he never had it at King's Land because by the time the telephone had penetrated rural Sussex he had begun to associate it with work and fatigue and hurry; whereas King's Land meant for him repose and home life—and Mamma did not need it.

My father used to make us delightful paper birds which flapped their wings and beautiful little paper boxes which fitted into each other. Later I learnt to make the little boxes cunningly folded to amuse my own children, but I always wanted to leave the magic of the flapping birds an unprobed secret. When I saw him by the lamp-light of King's Land making them for my children it still enthralled me as of old.

My mother had the view from their drawing-room in Cheyne Walk painted by Grace Joel, a charming scene of the river with the brown-sailed barges of that date and the misty grey of a wintry London. This picture hangs in the King's Land drawing-room.

It was from Cheyne Walk that my father started for France when he walked from Toul to Rome through the early summer weeks of 1901. We have the letters and the postcards which he sent Mamma during that famous and miraculous walk, all of which she preserved most carefully.

In the June of 1902 H.B. found us all rooms in the little farm of Godsmark at the south end of Ashurst Common. That was the first time I heard the cuckoo and the first time I saw my father riding a bicycle; and here too Phil Kershaw became a vivid part of our lives. Young, Irish and gay, he had been my father's friend at Balliol and became his companion in many adventures on land and sea. They arrived at Godsmark as we were going to bed and the quiet of the garden and farmhouse broke into noise and life as they joined Mamma at the end of the long stone-flagged path. They had parcels of food, bottles of wine, newspapers and happy faces. My father's dark curly hair was damp with sweat when he took off his hat and scratched his head, and Phil Kershaw, lithe and delightful, had a black eye because of a fall from his bicycle the day before.

Another of H.B.'s visits one afternoon coincided with Elizabeth, my baby sister, pulling over the sewing machine and the small table it stood upon—no mean feat for an infant of only eighteen months! Nannie was making clothes for us in the garden under the apple trees—Louis and I were fighting each other as usual and Elizabeth was tottering around near the insecure sewing table when, with a heave-ho, down it came with a dull thud on the grass. Her baby sobs and cries were only from fear, for she was uninjured, and I was astonished that her face was not covered in blood. However, her Guardian Angel had seen that the heavy Singer sewing machine had fallen clear of her. Louis and I ceased fighting for five minutes and ran to welcome Papa. (Many years later at King's Land, when we were really wicked, Mamma told me that we children seemed to combine our most devilish achievements at the very moment that horse and trap brought my father home around the corner of the house from the Southwater–London train.)

H.B. brought Louis a delightful toy model of a cabby's whip while

H.B. (1902)

at Ashurst. Louis cracked and played with it, to my nervous apprehension, and it was often used by him to quell my revolting habit of teasing. I remember thinking it was a just revenge on his part.

The golden days of the Ashurst holiday came to an end just as the haymaking began in mid-June and we all returned to 104 Cheyne Walk, where my brother Hilary was born in August. We called him "Blue Boy" because when Louis and I first saw him he was swaddled in a blue shawl.

In that winter of 1902 Elizabeth was given a small birthday party in the nursery. My father came up unexpectedly at the end of the festivities and gave her a very large illustrated edition of Robert Louis Stevenson's *A Child's Garden of Verses*. A great hush fell upon us—so large a book for such a little girl. My mother took care of it and used to read us some of the verses now and again in the drawing-room. 'Good-bye to the farm' and 'The Lamp-Lighter' meant a lot to me.

One day, the lady next door was seriously ill and two jolly great men arrived with a huge hay-cart laden with mountains of golden straw which, to our great delight, they began to toss all over the road opposite the sick lady's house. It was to deaden the rumble and rattle of the noisy iron wheels and horses' hoofs of passing traffic on the stone metalled road (before the wooden blocks were in use). I think only the rich could afford this luxury in London. When the time arrived for our walk, no sooner were we out of the little garden gate than we plunged like barking seals into the delightful golden depths of the straw! How right children are! God made the world and its produce for our delight. Nannie's alarm was most impressive—we were all hauled back to the pavement, retrieving hoops and gloves and tam-o'-shanters, and told that the highway was no thoroughfare for little children, and that our highly pitched, squeaking glee would disturb the poor sick lady. It was a forsaken glory to leave behind that golden lake of brittle straw, but we forgot almost at once in Battersea Park, where we busily collected defenceless wood-lice which rolled themselves into slate-coloured balls as we dropped them gently 'plop! plop!' into the dark waters of the gridded caverns of the park drains. I have since comforted myself in discovering that all sturdy wood-lice can swim at a pinch—but it was a cruel deed and I knew it for such.

Better for our souls were the Battersea walks in May when we innocently collected the fallen blossoms from the chestnut trees and arrayed them in patterns of immature design or put them in our handkerchiefs and smuggled them home to the nursery, where they were discovered to be brown, tired and bruised from the pockets of our little reefer coats. Our companions in these childish escapades were sometimes Jock Tweed's three children, Lettice Elliot, or the four Walton children. Our Nannies had endless conversations about their own interests and affairs, but they were excellent guardians and knew by unfailing instinct and the watchful eye if we were 'doing wrong'.

For a few weeks late in the summer of 1903 Mamma and Papa rented 'Bleak House' at Slindon, and we all moved down in a body by train to Barnham Junction and thence by hired trap to Slindon.

Annie the cook and Clara the Irish housemaid went before to prepare for the invasion. My father did a good deal of writing there that summer and I remember he showed us the English Channel, blue and mysterious far away to the south, from the garden, because Slindon is on the first slopes of the Downs. That summer when he was sailing from Littlehampton he dropped a heavy block on his left foot and had to rest it a great deal. Mamma used to dress the wound, and I remember thinking how large and white his foot was.

Frances and Gilbert Chesterton came to stay nearby for a few days and called at Bleak House. Gilbert and H.B. seemed to talk the whole time. We children could not understand one word of the torrent. H.B. was lying on the lawn with head pillowed on his arm. Talk, talk, talk! We heard it through the bushes, where we were up to mischief as usual. Elizabeth had now joined Louis and me for fun in the garden and Hilary was a year old.

My grandmother, Madame Belloc, lived a little way down the village street from Bleak House near the Newburgh Arms in a long low cottage with a fine view of the sea, and on exceptionally clear days you could see France from her south verandah—which used to make her very sentimental. We used to run in to see her through her open French window accompanied by Emily the nursemaid, who wore demure black clothing and a straw sailor hat. Grannie would welcome us with cries of delight—'Oh my dears—my little dears'. She was in ample black silk clothing with white lace over her silver hair, and although pleased to welcome us was a little fearful for her many precious personal possessions, of which the room seemed thronged. We were short in stature, but keen and eager, stretching out our childish hands towards her many bright treasures. I particularly loved the little miniature set in pearls, of my father as an infant, and after Grannie died my Aunt Marie * gave it to me and it has always been a special possession. It was from this same cottage in the March of 1924 that she took her peaceful leave of this life at the remarkable age of ninety-six, and was buried in the small graveyard of St Richard's Catholic Church in the village.

Grannie Belloc had always led a very active life, and when a young woman her wealthy father had given her a generous allowance and her freedom to travel. She had written several books about the people she met and about her travels.

In the early years of her old age she found sometimes that Slindon seemed dull, in spite of having several friends in the village. Then she would hire the cab from the village, drive to Barnham station and take the train to London, where she would go to Westminster and see my Aunt Marie. This was a great anxiety because Grannie much enjoyed going about London in the horse omnibuses. She found it vastly more interesting and would not take cabs, and as she advanced in years it was not very safe for her, but she never had a misadventure and people always responded to the deep, kindly interest she took in her surroundings and those she met. She was delightfully unselfconscious and never shy—her excellent eyesight and hearing lasted right to the very end of her life, two of God's many blessings with which He endowed her. The water-colours she painted were excellent and Victorian. This was her only craft: her gifts and talents were entirely intellectual. She did not make things or embroider, and her shapely, interesting hands had obviously never known manual use.

When writing letters at her beautiful little desk in Slindon she used a quill as her father had done before her, and I can hear the 'scratch,

* Mrs Belloc Lowndes, my father's only sister and nearly two years his senior. She married Frederick Lowndes, who for many years was on the staff of *The Times*.

scratch' of it now as we waited for her to finish her letters. She wrote to her daughter Marie every day, but I believe this was the custom of those days. A dry little cough seemed to be a constant nuisance to her, and she told me she had never thrown it off ever since the time she caught pneumonia when a young woman.

It seemed to me that she was always dressed in good, stiff, black silk or satin, which rustled. In the days of her youth and wealth she must have been the despair of her dressmaker because she would never pinch in her waist, as was the fashion, and she always refused to wear corsets of any sort. This greatly distressed her mother, Eliza Parkes, who thought it wanton eccentricity. As a family, our personal appearance has been a secondary consideration. We have other forms of vanity instead.

I wish I had known her as a young woman, because from the books she wrote she sounds so gay, active and observant. Her little book of poems, all written and published by the time she was twenty-six, are a delightful insight into her young mind and heart. One is about galloping across the downs near Hastings, and her relish for the exhilaration is a tribute to the zest for life which she handed on to my father in such great measure. Although not yet a Catholic, she portrays a very religious spirit in some of these poems. As a child she had been taken to the city of London to watch the procession for the Duke of Wellington's funeral, and she writes a narrative verse about the experience echoing the national sentiments of the time. She used to tell us children about this episode as it had naturally made a great impression on her childish emotions.

When we returned to 104 Cheyne Walk my father was deep in arranging and writing *Avril*, his book about French Renaissance poetry, and was lecturing up and down England on his French Revolution studies with his vast collection of lantern slides. All the slides of the Revolution battles were from his own diagrams and drawings. They lived in small, strong, wooden boxes, and for many years I remember 'slide boxes' as being part of our life; they came and went like the inevitable baggage of life and travel, and were to be seen in the hall on the table or being carried to the waiting cab or arriving by 'Messenger Boy' (that most excellent service for the prosperous or busy Londoner of those days. I believe 'The Messenger Office' Service has gone with many other good things.) My father would often hold some slides against the light for us, much to our awe and delight, but although I could discern nothing at all it seemed most entertaining and important. Looking at the slide boxes yesterday after over fifty years, I see how beautifully they were made and how each slide has a perfectly fitted wooden compartment.

In the late autumn of 1903 we had our famous nursery fire. It was in the evening and the nursery maid in some incompetent way exploded the bottle of methylated spirit with which she was filling a small stove. Hilary was the baby in the wicker cradle on the floor, Elizabeth and I were in bed in the night nursery next door, Nannie was down in the basement kitchen, and Mamma had just come in from a party. I woke with the noise of sundry alarming sounds; there were hurried footsteps and orders given in frightened voices. Suddenly our door flew open wide, the passage light streamed in and Mamma, in a long silk dress and with her hat on, swept in followed by Annie the cook.

Coming to my bed, Mamma said gently, 'Up quickly, darling,' and taking a blanket from the bed wrapped me in it, while Annie the cook was collecting Elizabeth and wrapping her in one too. All my alarm went. This was fun! This was adventure! We were hurried out into the passage, down the stairs, and into the front hall, where we met Nannie with baby Hilary bundled in a shawl and Louis in a dressing-gown. We all went out into the night to the house of a friendly neighbour three doors away. Later Elizabeth and I were highly commended for our prompt obedience in not resisting our rescue!

When poor Mamma returned immediately to her house the fire engines had arrived and a vast crowd of local folk from Milman Street and Cheyne Walk thronged the road, the pavement and the gate, where a huge policeman barred the front door. The poor from Milman Street let her through the crush and press but the policeman told Mamma she could not enter the house. She was so distressed and anxious that her voice failed her and the poor pressed forward saying, 'She is the lady of this house. She is our friend—let her in, she is Mrs Belloc.' Whereupon the astonished bobby let her in. The fire was under control and the drenched nursery room was smouldering and in ruins, but the flames had not spread. For many years a completely charred chest of drawers was kept in the scullery here as a souvenir and Mamma had Masses said in thanksgiving because it might have been far worse and all were safe. Hilary's wicker cot had caught fire almost at once and Nannie told me that my blue summer felt bonnet had roasted brown in its box on a shelf. This seemed very remarkable to me. I think my father was away that night. I cannot remember him.

We children all went away to Pixton, at the kind invitation of Lady Carnarvon, while the nursery was cleaned, redecorated and refurbished. Clara the housemaid came with Nannie to help look after us because the poor little nursery maid had been dismissed at Nannie's request. It was at Pixton that I first saw a stag and was somewhat affrighted. There was also a jolly cockatoo who lived a well-fed secluded life—I have forgotten his name but he was fun, with his yellow crest, piercing eye and curious noises. He had a great perch on a metal stand.

Mr Reginald Blunt bought 104 Cheyne Walk in the autumn of 1904, much to my parents' distress because it meant moving away and they had become very fond of the little house. But for some time they had been contemplating buying a house of their own somewhere in Sussex. We stayed on until March 1905 and my brother Peter was born in Cheyne Walk in October 1904. That winter my Uncle Garret McEnerney came to see us from California; he was the widower of my mother's sister Elizabeth who died in 1900 and the dear friend of her youth and her family. I was greatly impressed by the size of his massive head! And after he had gone away I asked for a page of newspaper and, spreading it on the floor, drew his head because our scribbling books were not big enough! We also rolled about the drawing-room carpet the golden sovereigns of which he had kindly given us one each—but this extravagant form of amusement was halted and after we had retrieved them from dark and inaccessible corners Mamma collected them and opened our first humble Post Office Savings Accounts with them.

Elodie Belloc and the children (1903)

12 *Sussex*

B Y the Easter of 1905 we were all installed temporarily in Courthill Farm House, Slindon, Sussex, with most of the family belongings—a hired home until Mamma and Papa found the right house to buy and could establish a country home for us all in Sussex. Courthill was a reasonably sized house for a family and five children. We were told some years later that it was haunted by ghosts of smugglers, and I once asked Mamma 'who was the little lady with the red shawl round her shoulders who went through the doors without opening them?' And once, too, Elizabeth saw a large phantom dog sitting on the end of her little bed! My father's study was an excellent attic in the high quiet of the roof approached by a little, narrow, winding staircase, with two windows and a celestial southern view over the trees towards the sea eight or nine miles away beyond the cornfields and the sloping plain. We were bathed in great tin hip baths and water was brought upstairs in large steaming cans. Elizabeth and I were too large now to go into the bath together, which created the eternal problem of who went first to bed—with the overpowering reluctance in childhood to leave the garden and its unsupervised delights on summer evenings, or the joyous circumstance of winter with no Nannie-in-the-Nursery while she put the two baby boys to bed! Our downstairs playroom had an overflow of 'grown-ups'' books which we explored endlessly with a seemingly tireless concentration and repetition, and when we found one with illustrations we told each other stories built up by our immature minds from the pictures and pretended to read the text as the grown-ups read to us in the evenings. Fifty years ago many more books were illustrated than now. We formed a deep disgust for any books lacking this great aid to entertainment and dubbed them rubbish.

Soon after our arrival at Courthill H.B. bought a mare called 'Monster', a steady sturdy chestnut cob who was an immense joy and excitement to us. A raleigh cart also arrived—it was the height of bliss when Mamma drove us to Arundel or over to Ford to see the Balfours and on summer picnics up Vale Bottom beyond Dale Park. My father used sometimes to ride 'Monster' up on the Downs and before his setting forth there was a great send off—the spurs on his boots were my special joy, I could just reach them after he mounted and used to twirl round the little spiked wheels. He had elastic loops fitted to the end of his fawn-coloured covert trousers which went under his instep. He said that horses were a stupid sort of animal but a worthy enough mount for man. He was frightened of their uncertain behaviour, as indeed we all were.

Allan the groom made Louis a bow of hazel with arrows, a source of fun, fighting and competition; and my father with great skill made us delightful whistles of ash. He learnt that as a boy. With some secret grasp he worked off the young rind from spring saplings some $\frac{3}{4}$ inch thick and 6 to 8 inches long, having shaped the mouthpiece first of all at the wider end and cut out the notches for the notes at intervals of about $\frac{1}{2}$ inch. This seemed to take a long time to execute, so great was our impatience to start making piercing and intolerable noises! I wonder if there is any man or boy left in Sussex who can still make these local whistles in season?

In the late spring of that year, 1905, my Aunt Julia Hopkins, Mamma's eldest sister, came to visit us from San Francisco, California. This was her first visit to England, and she seemed to us children strangely enthusiastic about country life and experiences, but when we took her to the orchard to see the chickens we were appalled how cruelly stung she was by the nettles which stood in threatening, treacherous ranks waist high and which we ourselves avoided from past experience. She was most generous to us, buying us dolls and chocolates and making us pretty clothes. She also taught me how to read and write; strangely enough, I delighted in her lessons. She brought with her from America a little reading book with pictures and stories which caught my attention—each line of print had beneath the same sentence in clear script. I learnt very quickly.

The Slindon Catholic Church was only two fields away from Court-hill up an extremely steep hillside, which sloped eastward from the front garden because the house lay in a valley or wide hollow of the

Downs foothills. Once Elizabeth, Louis and I scampered away, hot and untidy from the garden, up the hillside grass and flowers—those two fields seemed interminable—and when we reached the low flint wall of the little graveyard we heaved, pushed and pulled each other over, leaving buttons and hair ribbons behind, and fell into the quiet of the dead! Having had high jinks among the mounds and tombstones, I then insisted that Louis should hold me up to kiss our Lord's feet on the huge stone crucifix in the middle of the graveyard. This act of piety greatly bored Louis, who, being a boy, was made of sterner stuff. I then crept into the unlocked church and was alarmed and frightened to find it quiet with an unearthly quiet and a most unfamiliar emptiness because I had only known it on Sundays at the second Mass when it was well peopled and full of the rustles, smiles and whispers of a friendly congregation (and the fun of watching Grannie put half a crown into the collection plate and take out sixpence, an old French custom!). I tip-toed out and told Louis and Elizabeth that I was off home, as it was dawning on me that the whole escapade had been unruly and out of order. So we scrambled breathlessly over the wall, topped the brow for the descent home and heard coming from the valley the long anxious calling of the grown-ups who had marked our absence. When the reprimanding, scolding and troubles began I recounted with smug priggishness how I had kissed the crucifix and entered the church and said prayers, which made such an unforeseen impression that we were all three let off punishment on condition that we asked permission the next time we felt the call to prayer!

It was in this church that Louis first served Mass in blue cassock and white cotta, having been taught the Latin responses by Fr. Wheelhan. It gave my father such pleasure that Sunday that he seemed overjoyed and, following Louis into the sacristy after Mass, brought him out into the church and gave him a golden sovereign, while we all began to hop about like happy fleas—because Mass had seemed so long!

The lane down to Courthill lay at the extreme end of the village and went steeply down through a wooded incline with an overgrown disused chalk pit on the right. This pit was then used, from ancient custom, as the village 'tip', wherein all the village rubbish was disposed of. All the old boots, kettles, broken china, battered buckets and rusty scuttles fascinated us children, but any scavenging was strictly forbidden us by Nannie. I remember a delectable small blue enamel saucepan there which I longed to possess—its handle lay towards my hand most invitingly. Those were the days of greater cottage thrift and economy, with poverty and compost heap in the villages of England—so there was no horror or stench about this tip. But now it is all cleared away and the beautiful dell is given over to beech nuts and leaves.

Charles and Elizabeth Lowndes, our cousins, would sometimes come to see us if they were staying with Grannie, and we sometimes called on them at her cottage. They used to bring a lot of toys with them from London, and these were laid out on the sofa in the dining-room; Charles most generously asked me to take my choice and Elizabeth gave me a book which I still possess and cherish. One day I asked Charles if he would marry me when I grew up and he solemnly 'turned me down' with wisdom beyond his six years, saying, with intense preoccupation, that first cousins could not marry! We were busy at the moment in a ditch collecting green slime on sticks while our nurses exchanged gossip!

Once Aunt Julia brought some glorious golden wild broom into the house, which frightened and annoyed my father as he was very superstitious and said it was most unlucky. She, never having heard of this and being entranced by the blossom, did not readily give in to what seemed to her unreasonable, so my father became quite threatening and won the argument, as Aunt Julia reluctantly took the broom out into the garden. We thought the whole episode of flashing eyes and fear and authority among the grown-ups a fine entertainment. Such a nice change to see a grown-up Aunt being ordered to obey!

Christmas of 1905 was passed at Slindon and poor Peter, only fourteen months old, had scarlet fever. The dining-room was turned into an isolation sick-room with a great white disinfected sheet hanging over the door, and Nannie nursed him. We used to pay him visits, consumed with morbid curiosity, through the two windows. He always looked cheerful and never scarlet.

Mr Josiah Wedgwood, a neighbour in the village, gave a children's party at which I was given a charming Japanese doll with ink-black hair and slanty eyes in kimono and wide sash. Showing this to Mamma next morning, she exclaimed, 'Oh, a little pagan doll for a little Catholic girl!' From the tone of her voice and the expression on her face, I felt the doll fall steeply in my estimation, so with calm determination I took it upstairs to Nannie's bedroom and, grasping it firmly by the legs, whacked its poor head a mighty crack on the brass knob of Nannie's bed, the shattered plaster flying all over the room. Alas! Mamma was not pleased at such a violent act of destruction. I thought she would have been delighted. It is very hard to please!

Some weeks of the summer of 1906 were spent at Port de l'Arche with Mrs Leigh-Smith while King's Land was being prepared and added to. My father came with us to see us through the journey and happily took Louis about the steamer to show him things. I was in such a state of bewildered awe that I clung to Mamma and stayed in the ladies' saloon among the red plush. I was momentarily diverted by the thick white lace antimacassars as they were a novelty.

We must have been a *corvée* for Mrs Leigh-Smith: five children and a nurse and nursemaid. It seemed a long stay, but I do not remember how long. I got homesick for Mamma, although Mrs Leigh-Smith was exceedingly kind to us and had us given swimming lessons in the Seine by a large, kindly, strong French lady. We splashed from a boat on a sandbank in the wide Seine with a rope round our middle, which was a necessary discomfort for safety, and picked luscious strawberries in the garden and played tents and 'Napoleon's campaign' in the beautiful blue-canopied bed. I became so rough and wild with excitement that I had to be temporarily banished to sleep in the nursemaid's room in a delightful attic. From here I then climbed out on to the roof and saw from the parapet the wide world lie beneath me far below, and a vast flock of sheep come moving by through the white Normandy dust—something I had only seen in books. I was in a fairyland of delight until the shepherd saw me and became hysterical with terror and the well-reasoned certainty that I was out of place and would pitch forward and fall to the road. He shouted and pointed in great alarm so that I became suddenly frightened, aware of the danger I was in, and crept back. We went for heavenly picnics with Mrs Leigh-Smith along the banks of the cool, wide Seine, and Louis used to watch the occasional French trains go thundering by over the first great girder bridge we had ever seen.

When we returned to England, we went to Bognor into lodgings as King's Land was not quite ready to receive us. When at last the great day arrived, we took train to Billingshurst, where we were met by the miller, Mr Powell, and Bernard Wood with two country farm carts, and, loaded in with luggage and wonder, went slowly through those beautiful narrow lanes of the Sussex of fifty years ago. Through the sunlit evening, by Coolham and round a bend in a lane, suddenly the mill towered above the hedges and field—and there lay King's Land by the road with the long shadows from the oaks around. We were home, and my father helped to lift us from the carts. We rushed round in a delirium of delight and found Annie the cook and Tipper the dog and all our toys and familiar furniture from which we had been separated for so long.

King's Land had once been a village shop, and we found the store rooms at the south end had been made into a nursery wing with a schoolroom, bathroom and two night nurseries. The house cast a warm, embracing enchantment upon me. My father showed us his study, which seemed a long way from the nursery end. The drawing room, which had been the shop, was barely arranged and was waiting for the red material which my father brought from France to clothe the walls instead of wallpaper, and the shelves which once held ginghams and cotton prints were empty and waiting for the unpacking and arranging of the great boxes of books.

Our schoolroom had been the shop's bacon room. Great hooks were still in the ceiling, which we thought most distinguished, and we always hung our Christmas decorations from them—a series of complicated coloured paper chains.

My father's study lay several rooms away from us, almost the length of the house, and was approached through the dining-room. Its walls were clothed in lovely French material with a pattern of dark and light green leaves against which his pictures looked delightful. It had a red carpet on the floor. His writing table lay before the window and on this, among his many belongings, stood a large crucifix. It was in this room that Mr James Gunn, my father's dear friend, painted the portrait of him which hangs in the Union at Oxford. The round table in this picture, which is made of iron and is cunningly painted to represent rosewood, belonged to our great-grandfather, Joseph Parkes. There was a passing fashion for these tables a hundred years ago when England was the great ironmaster of the world.

This room was sacred to his work and hard-driven, willing secretaries. We were not supposed to go in without knocking or permission. It was a splendid storehouse of writing things and coloured inks—also 'bull's-eye' peppermints. On a small table stood the Remington typewriter—this never interested me, but my brother Louis greatly enjoyed occasional permission to tap out his name on carbon paper. One day when my father was away from home, hearing it was the birthday of Ruby Goldsmith, the secretary, we paid her a call in the study bringing as a sincere gift a small pail of pond water containing a few reluctant orange-bellied newts. She turned quite pale from shock, and her breathless London inexperience of Sussex pond life was sad to see. We were so sorry to have thus upset her—her distress was so evident that we took them away quite happily. When I met her *forty years* afterwards in New York she remembered the whole incident vividly with almost the same horror.

By Christmas of our first year there, 1906, we had become acquainted with several local children and Mamma wanted us to have a Christmas tree and party. The drawing-room was not yet in order nor was the hall built, so Mamma asked Mr Powell, the miller, if she could have it in the first compartment of the Mill. He and Bernard Wood cleared all the sacks of grain to one side and stacked them together, the great scales were run into a corner, the glorious cobwebs were all brushed down and away and the tree was put near the middle post and decorated. This room of the mill is the first one from the ground floor and is reached by a wide-footed, strong, ladder-type of stair. It gives the impression of being a circular room but is really six-sided.

All the final arrangements were kept a great secret from us. After tea we all put on our coats and, holding hands, followed Mamma out into the December darkness, she carrying a lantern and Nannie Drewitt carrying Peter. There seemed little shoving or pushing as we were full of awe and expectation because Mamma said Father Christmas had chosen an unusual place for his tree.

When we arrived in the mill yard there was light coming through the mill door and a storm-lantern hanging outside. Bernard and Papa helped us all up the rough ladder as, with breathless excitement, we arrived—and there was the tree glowing with candles, twinkling tinsel and coloured balls, with a heavenly smell of oatmeal flour and candles all together and heaps of room for ragging round. We all pushed and shoved, with cries of delight, and there were dark corners into which one could push the smaller children in our attacks of excited happiness! We patted the great full sacks of grain and put our arms round their packed fullness in the light of the candles. I was given a delectable blue satin bag of chocolates which seemed a celestial climax to a perfect evening. I offered one to Papa. He was near the tree staring at it wide-eyed and far away. He did not at first hear me in the happy youthful hum and din of squealing children, but when he did he bent and put a large hand into the bag, coming out of some far dream! He thanked me warmly, stroked my face and put the chocolate into his mouth; and I longed to know what it had for a 'centre'! But I saw he was 'far away' again and looking at the tree with a rapt expression—I wonder what he was thinking about?

A few round games were organized, crackers were pulled and toys dropped, mislaid and looked for with laughter and tears; then we became rough and abandoned and had to be quelled until, alas! the party came to an end. We went back to the house by lantern light, then off to bed to hang up our stockings.

A constant flow of visitors seemed to come to King's Land. We watched them arrive or take leave from our schoolroom window, climbing into or out of the 'dogcart' trap which took them to or from Southwater railway station, with their luggage and bowler hats or boater straw hats or caps or long skirts and flowered hats and veils.

John Phillimore was one of the first visitors. He came of a naval family—both his father and his eldest brother were admirals—and had been a close friend of my father's when they were both up at Oxford. Eventually he became head of the Classical department at Glasgow

University. He bicycled over from his home at Shedfield in Hampshire, arriving cool and collected in beautiful tweeds and hand-knit stockings. It was he who helped H.B. to panel the dining-room in new oak which was later rubbed with linseed oil and beeswax. Beer was consumed and songs were sung—and Mr Aubrey Harding, the Coolham carpenter, came later to finish it for them! It was, to us, an unfamiliar sight to see them in shirt-sleeves, puffing and blowing as they sawed planks of oak and laid down the law! We left the long, low room marvelling.

Charles Somers Cocks was one of our favourite guests. He had been at the Oratory School with H.B. and, having been boys together, they were wholly delightful to listen to as their ragging intimacy was the height of entertainment to us. Somers Cocks was a Foreign Office official—he was highly intelligent and informed, with no ambition whatever. He gave my brother Louis a magnificent four-foot-long telescope, from which my father showed us the moon and stars at night and the Downs by day. When my father had a Ford car Mr Cocks seemed a constant companion, wrapped in a big coat and pouring out a stream of exciting talk as H.B. racketed us about the lanes and roads of England—in and out of hotels, in and out of beautiful cathedrals.

Once I met H.B. and Mr Cocks walking and talking along White Hall, the top lane of the parish. I was meandering slowly on a bicycle and they were so entirely engrossed in conversation that they never so much as saw me. It was the only genuine case of its kind I have encountered, though I have heard of such concentration. And I have often pondered since that the talk and intellectual pursuits of those days had a depth and quality which I shall never meet again. It is the salt of life, and has deserted our society because we have neglected it.

Cecil Chesterton and Maurice Baring came frequently also in those early days. Cecil's and H.B.'s talk was all political and endless; but Maurice's subjects were very various. He spoke more jerkily in short statements, and sometimes would walk rapidly from the room for no apparent reason. Cecil would talk to us with a pleasing solemnity, but Maurice organized delightfully rough games and we often rode on his back, either with him on all fours on the drawing-room floor rapidly in and out of the furniture, or at great and dangerous speed round the garden. He dearly loved a frolic and enjoyed our answering delight. His eyes were shining and he allowed us to stroke his bald head.

Mr Wilfrid Blunt occasionally drove the three miles to call on my mother and father, with two Arab ponies and Teddy Roberts the groom with him, but more often Mamma and Papa went up to his house, New Buildings, on Sunday evenings to dine. George Wyndham, who was Mr Blunt's cousin, came once or twice to call while he was staying at New Buildings, and I thought him so enchantingly gracious and beautiful that I hung about the front railings for a very long time, thinking that a god had called. And one Sunday morning he arrived riding a large strong white donkey which Mr Blunt had brought over from Egypt. This was beyond all the dreams of Paradise, and we were so awed that we forgot to ask for a ride. H.B. was so delighted to see Mr Wyndham that he gave a great shout of welcome and after a good deal of discussion and greetings the donkey was led away by our groom to the stables. Into the house they plunged and the inevitable torrent of talk and gay laughter poured out to us, the uncorking of wine and clink of glasses joining the merriment.

The afternoon that 'Hal' Fisher arrived was wintertime, and being in the midst of many other visits he had a very large quantity of luggage—bags and portmanteaux of various shapes and sizes. We children returning at that time from our walk were delighted to see the front terrace strewn with bags, and as there was some hitch or hold-up in the opening of the front door, we nipped in among the baggage and began to 'play at porters', which only means chucking other people's belongings all over the place! 'Hal' Fisher was so happy that down he went in bended fashion and danced the most perfect frog dance we had ever seen. Shouting with joy, the hurling of luggage became wilder and wilder until suddenly Mamma and a maid appeared and the whole carnival halted, discipline was restored, and winter hats were sorted out. We were solemnly introduced to Mr Fisher and banished in a rosy glow to our own quarters. But there were two more treats in store, because after tea 'Hal' Fisher told us a story and before he went away he danced the frog dance again for us. I thought he was a darling

—so thin and agile and seemingly tall, with such a kindly eye. He is fixed for ever in my reel of memories.

Mamma and Papa had obtained an altar, tabernacle and a big missal with its oak stand for the chapel from Mr and Mrs Reginald Balfour when they left Ford, where they had a chapel, and the first Mass was said in our chapel in 1907 by Father Xavier, the Father Prior from Storrington. Papa served and made loud responses and Mamma seemed very happy and wept a little. I think it was winter or spring because Elizabeth and I wore new little fluffy blue capes which had come from France. They were inadequate and I felt rather cold. The chapel was dark in those days, as the altar and tabernacle lay across the window, but the candles glowed and there was a mysterious intimacy about the Sacred Rites—and oh joy, no sermon!

The confessional was a very heavy clumsy folding wooden screen which lived in the large old fireplace of the chapel when not in use and was erected with a good deal of banging and rattling—it was a great conjecture to us next door in the nursery what the grown-ups were confessing.

When the war of 1939 was declared and the blacking-out of windows became law, we moved the altar to the south wall so as to manage the blind each night. This made the chapel much lighter, so we left it there when the war ended and the hateful 'black-outs' came down all over the country. My father was the only man in England who truly relished and approved of the 'black-out'. He said that in our climate all windows should be heavily curtained by sundown. Wars or no wars, on a winter's evening he would shut out the most beautiful after-glow or even sometimes the long summer light of June nights. But this was because he felt the cold, and also King's Land has a public footpath very near the windows from which you can see into our living-room, and the stranger passing, if he wished, could see and jeer—not that I ever knew the passing stranger to be anything but most courteous and well behaved.

Miss Ruby Goldsmith, my father's secretary, came in 1908 and stayed with us for over fourteen years, dealing somehow with his phenomenal torrent of correspondence, appointments, essays, lectures, books and journalism, and also the ceaseless filing of letters, manuscripts and the faithful keeping of his memoranda, about which he was most energetic and concerned. 'Oh, Miss Goldsmith, put that down for me!' my father would say.

One day H.B. brought from London a quantity of large sheets of red and white tissue paper and a small roll of fine wire, and we were summoned and told the delightful news that Papa was going to make a paper balloon. Tremendous scurrying of helpers of all sorts took place, scissors were brought, and on the dining-room table H.B. cut out a number of gores and glued them together with great ingenuity —alternate stripes of rustling red and white. He secured one end of the joined gores round a small circular wire frame and the opposite ends were fixed by a round paper cap sealing the joins. All this took some time and we tiptoed in and out, getting bored ourselves with H.B.'s most impressive concentration. When it was finished the glue had to dry; and eventually a lamp was brought and lit and we all went out into the field, the balloon being carried with care. Three people held its top and one held the wired mouth over the hot air from the lamp while my father gave loud instructions how not to let it burn—all his precious hours of work! Then the magic began of its filling and swelling. By now it was evening; it looked like an enchanted great pumpkin, and began to sway and strain to be off as the hot air made it lighter and lighter. When it was completely inflated, my father fixed a large fluff of cotton wool to the wire frame. Soaked in methylated, this was lighted and H.B. cried, 'She can be released'—and up, up, up it went into the evening sky, away above the oaks off towards Billingshurst. Witnessing this simple marvel of science and H.B.'s ingenious industry was a great moment in our lives.

He made several other balloons and one, to our huge delight, caught fire and burst into flames very soon after release, the flaming cotton wool falling to the earth like a fiery dart from heaven.

In 1909 my mother and father bought a sturdy New Forest pony. When Mr Powell brought him along we asked H.B. what was its name and he said at once, 'Oh, we shall call the beast Rawcus because he is a little horse.' This joke was entirely lost on me because I had never heard the phrase 'a raucous voice'. As soon as Louis had learnt to ride, H.B. said, 'Ah, you have won your spurs', and the next time he returned from London he brought Louis some small spurs—these I greatly envied.

The night nursery window with bars looked down into the garden behind the house. Immediately below lay Mamma's 'little' garden where the lilies grew in summer and her small red-tiled platform stood, and on some warm fine summer evenings the grown-ups dined there, to our dreamy entertainment. We sucked up a lot of silent joy from their happy talk and laughter. Having tiptoed to the window and secretly looking down on them, we saw great dishes of food handed round and glistening morsels of ice popped into the golden wine. It all seemed specially wonderful, as it was a stolen secret pleasure to look upon them so engrossed and lively, our quizzing eyes and ears unknown to them; an invisible audience of hazy drowsy childhood.

Across the little river Adur running through our field my father had a wooden dam built with strong oaken posts and a sluice, so that a delightful natural swimming pool swelled on one side between the greasy clay banks. All through the summer holidays in all weathers it seems to have been a constant pleasure to us to plunge about and swim and splash. With rapturous shouts and cries we ran our young local friends down the sloping field into the dear muddy depths of the Adur, where we held 'aquatic sports' of an ill-assorted kind—in spite of the wails and protests of governesses and the neighbouring mammas. Those were the days of happy dim 'hygiene', gone forever now with the tiled, pagan swimming pools in all the corners of our dear England.

There was a small awe-inspiring incident when Hilary, my brother, fell from the dam into the deep side and Desmond MacCarthy calmly slid down the bank, waded in waist-deep and brought him out. It seemed a breathtaking and heroic act. He went on talking to H.B. all the time as if nothing was happening!

It was strictly forbidden to climb about the King's Land roofs, which were a Paradise of varied gullies and eaves—I think there are nine gables—but this rule, I now regret to say, was always broken if an opportunity came along. One early summer morning I was enjoying myself almost to distraction in the main gully and paused to take a long penetrating look through the skylight down into the bedroom corridor below—lying flat along the lead and pressing my face against the glass.

To my frozen horror my father was there motionless and looking up. I was ordered off the roof at once but it took a bit of time before I could move. I had seen more than I bargained for, and was stunned with surprise. He was in his camel-hair dressing-gown with tousled hair, and magnificent in his just wrath; it was an unfamiliar angle to be viewing his upturned face from above. It was no tiddler minnow that I came across that early summer morning as I peered into the glassy pool. I was not punished later and, strangely enough, it was never referred to. I wonder if in the largeness of his heart the fearful astonishment on my face from a similarly unfamiliar place dispersed his extreme annoyance?

H.B. took a great interest in the garden, as vegetables and salads and fruit all cooked or dished in a French way meant such a lot to him, and he used to call the garden the 'estate'. He did no gardening, but gave orders to and took the advice of his gardener, Frank Laker, who was with him for forty devoted years. Laker was born and nurtured in Shipley and lived at Dragon's Green. He was tall and strongly built and my mother told us he was Quasind. Sometimes you would hear my father calling very loudly from my mother's little red-tiled terrace, 'Laker, where are you?', and his shout would echo back from mill and village church and roll round the roofs of King's Land. Laker's answering 'Sir' would be a target for H.B., who would set off in that direction at immense speed, and then a torrent of orders would be given and advice taken. Asparagus, cos lettuce and aubergine were grown with great success, among many other things, but Laker's real pride was the onion bed. The whole garden and its produce was a miracle of care and a glory to see, and woe betide if we played 'bears' between the rows of lovely peas or raided the cucumber frame or made umbrellas from the rhubarb. My mother with other local help attended to the small flower garden, but she and Laker were tremendous friends. He loved her charity, justice and sense of humour, and she delighted in his Sussex ways, his knowledge of the elements and his great physical strength. He used to tell me about it when he was an old man.

Early in the hot summer of 1911 I asked Mamma if I could have a bicycle. She was greatly perturbed but did not say no. She told me I was very young and small and that bicycling was harmful for little

132

girls, but she said, 'I will ask Papa about it—he knows best.' So she did, and he called over the fence by the schoolroom one day, 'My darling, I hear you want a bicycle—you shall have one, but from where can it be obtained?' Fluttering with excited expectation, I stuttered that there was one for sale at Coolham and that Percy Longhurst, the groom's boy, would bring it along for inspection. All these little cunning plans and secret inquiries had been hatched in hope and now were to be fulfilled. H.B. was like that—he always encouraged the desires of the young and was all for testing mechanical devices. Percy fetched it from Coolham and it was approved, although it was too big, but a very small saddle was obtained from Horsham. It was a genuine free wheel, very secondhand, and cost fifteen shillings, but had been repainted black rather roughly and had a quiet old-fashioned way about it! I positively worshipped it, and felt I now had the kingdom and the towns of the world within my reach. I never admitted to anyone how utterly exhausted I was after my first ride to Coolham with my father's friend, Mr Fernaux Mann, and how kind he was and pushed me up the hills. It was two miles there, with a drink of ginger-beer in the shop, and two miles home on a summer's evening.

Edith Rance said my sister Elizabeth could have a real child's bicycle if she wanted it from Dr Cox's handyman at the cottage near the blacksmith's. This we went to inspect, and Elizabeth found it to her liking. We rode it home and showed it to Mamma and Papa—and he gave Elizabeth the half-sovereign which was what it cost. It was far more solid than mine, with a fixed wheel and cork-covered handles.

My father quite soon said, 'I will take you to Steyning on our bicycles and there we will visit the brewery, which is famous, for you have never seen a brewery.' So we set off—he riding his beautiful, up-to-date 'Sunbeam oil bath' bicycle. All along the little white narrow lanes we went singing and rejoicing. It took a long time, and H.B. seemed in no mood for hurry. We went by Dial Post and Ashurst, passing Peppers and Capity, with only a few carts, horses and bicycles on the way, and H.B. saluted all the landsmen, a habit he handed on to us. I always greet landsmen and they always respond. At one point my father chose a curious short cut through a green lane, where we pushed our bumping rattling bicycles over rutty land with bullrushes

133

and grass hummocks; but it was exhausting and he said, 'Such short cuts are not worth it.' We were glad to find the flinty road again.

Alas! the brewery was shut when we arrived—I can't remember why. But we found a delightful man in the yard who took an order for a cask of beer to be sent to King's Land. And then, after resting at the White Horse Inn, and my father's ale and our ginger-beer, we set off home again, arriving tired but happy long after bed-time.

In his study my father wrote in front of the window, at a large table upon which, round his blotter, were arranged an enormous number of useful articles and gadgets of all sorts. They seemed countless—slide-rules, pens of every kind, colour and size, glorious scissors with long sharp points, many book-leaf cutters—one with a Voodoo's head with wicked glass eyes and one with a lizard's head—map measures with minute wheels which turned as you ran them over the paper and registered so many miles in scale, ashtrays, about four of them—one was painted in tinsel gold and said 'A present from Brighton', one was a lion's mouth yawning wide, and there was a splendid brass one with a centre made to hold a whole box of matches, erect and arranged so that you could select a match and strike it with ease. No one ever used the matches—I noticed the virgin unscratched surface of the emery board. This ashtray cost $6\frac{1}{2}d$.—I know this because I bought it in Horsham myself for Papa at the '$6\frac{1}{2}d$. Bazaar'. The delightful little scales for letter-weighing, so delicately balanced, were in front of the blotter, and just beyond them was the long row of lovely coloured inks—all colours, with a resplendent purple, a frowning Indian black, and a cheerful yellow. With Papa's permission we would sometimes select one, hold it to the light, and with a gentle shake dilute the colour against the side and squint at it, taking our childish delight in such simple things to bed with us—very often replenished with a sixpence or a new penny from his ever generous pocket. There were four candlesticks, two fashioned like bears dancing, the candle being fixed in the raised drinking goblet in their paws. I have never been able to capture the shining bright cleanliness of their shaggy coats and often wonder how Edie Rance kept all the crevices so radiant—but they still dance with a truly clumsy appearance, happy grins and lolling tongues, for in this world dance we must lest we be overtaken by

The table in the dining-room

some cheating melancholy, and if you ever have to sit long hours at work it is good to see dancing creatures on your work table. Besides all these possessions were sundry others, including many books of reference in a beautifully made little sloping support, and an oaken note-paper holder. Above all these stood the large black crucifix against the light: Compassion, Salvation, Beneficence forever.

When my father brought me from London a little working model of a sewing machine, I learnt the sad lesson that all mechanical devices must be conquered, understood, and looked after. I thought it would be easily worked—but alas, this was far from being the case! I soon lost heart when a rucked and grubby piece of stuff was removed by Nannie from an appallingly tangled ball of pink thread, with a broken needle somewhere in it all. However, it did inspire me to learn its use and really appreciate my beautiful efficient Singer many years later when I was nineteen years old. This he most generously gave me when, on leaving school, I wanted to make clothes of various kinds. I have it still, and if anything it is in better condition than all those thirty-five years ago when it came new and shining from the factory.

If the second week in June each summer promised to be fine, arrangements were made to cut our two fields of hay. Frank Laker and Ernest Powell would engage three or four other men, who arrived with scythes, whetstones, and small bundles of bread, cheese, and onions tied in spotted handkerchiefs. Cheerful and deliberate in their movements, they started to fell the wealth of grass and flowers in the two fields near the mill. With great sweeps and slow advance they moved along their individual swathes, happy masters of their craft, with an occasional stop to rest their backs and spit upon their hands to get a renewed grip upon the scythe. The swish of cutting and the musical rasp of honing broke the silence of the morning until we arrived after lessons to start playing noisily in the curving waves of fallen grass. If H.B. had not gone to London for work, he would remove his coat, take Bernard Wood's scythe, and swing along for one length of the field. His action was faster, more exhausting and more jerky than theirs, but we loved to watch him. Sweating and delighted, he would call for the enormous brown stone holder of beer which lay in the shade near the mill, all work ceased for ten minutes, glasses were brought, and everyone had a drink, with murmured thanks. Frank Laker would laugh and make a joke and, putting my nose to the uncorked beer jorum, I would inhale its happy acrid depths of wonder until my father shouted to me, 'Hi! stop that child!'

In the autumn of 1909 my father went to Nantes to order a vast hogshead of red wine and to arrange for its shipping to England. I think it was the ordinary wine of that Loire district, and it was laced with sturdy Algerian, as my father said it would travel better and be a more suitable drink for this climate—good body to it. He also told me about the wholesale merchant with whom he dealt. Alas! I have forgotten his name, but I could never forget that according to H.B. he slept with his boots and spurs on! Some weeks after H.B.'s return the wine arrived at Southwater station three miles away, and Ernest Powell's great blue hay-wain set out from Coolham to collect it and bring it to King's Land. Tremendous excitement prevailed upon its arrival, H.B. giving directions to Todman, our groom, and Frank Laker, who, with great strength and care and the help of Bernard Wood, rolled it cautiously down a ladder from the blue wain into the road, over the turf, through the back door into the kitchen yard and so through the lamp-room into the first of our three cellars. It was so set that it need not be disturbed again until the great day in springtime when it would be broached and bottled. The whole episode teemed with novelty, and surely it was the first great French barrel of wine to be housed in those ancient cellars?

I think we children must have been a great annoyance, hanging round watching the corking and the carrying of the bottles. My brother Hilary, being very young, was overcome by the strong fumes and had to be led away very white in the face to lie down! Half-way through the operation a bottle burst as my father was working the corking machine, and as he was holding the bottle at the time a jagged edge of broken glass pierced his left hand rather deeply near the base of his little finger. The doctor had to be fetched from Cowfold and three stitches were put in. When it was all healed he discovered the tendons of the little finger were severed, and after that it always lay shut against his palm, but it never seemed to worry him.

H.B.'s pipe smoking was a problem because when I was a child, in those long-ago days, a pipe smoked gave him pleasure but also made him feel a little sick. He smoked cherry-wood pipes and bought a whole new boxful at a time. He smoked pipes while working, but cigars after a meal. 'Black Cat' tobacco was his favourite for many years, until an American friend introduced him to 'Barking Dog' tobacco—because it 'did not bite'—and it made him less sick. This was purchased in America in quantities at a time. From the station would be brought a large wooden box lined with sealed tin, inside which were a number of 1-lb. tins sealed yet again, and on the paper wrapper of each was a mild dog barking with a friendly expression. I have never seen so much tobacco in a private house before or since, and never will again! But H.B. always bought everything in great generous amounts, whether it was shirts or drawing-pins, papers or socks—always by the dozen or the hundred.

When Cecil Chesterton stayed with us he smoked and coughed all the time, and if H.B. lit up his pipe as they walked about talking the crescendo of coughs was tremendous. We children used to listen fascinated and say, 'The great coughing competition is on' as racking explosion followed racking explosion and neither one nor the other could hear what they were saying, although they shouted above the din of their own coughing with great emphasis. The room became dim with smoke and the floor strewn with matches. They seemed quite unaware of our presence or their unusual behaviour! We ran away marvelling and delighted.

We now come to the Troll's Hut, which stands in a slightly elevated part of the kitchen garden and looks towards Chanctonbury and the South. It is built of wood and has a too ancient thatch of straw in which the birds have made havoc in places, so that it is none too rain-proof. My father built it in 1910 as a summer workroom and to house a great map of England which is fixed to the roof and pulls down like a giant sunblind. It is the 2 miles to the inch Ordnance Map, and was a constant joy to him when he began to plot our long cross-country routes when motoring. It is a fine sight to see the straight Roman roads running like ruled lines in various parts of England, and the Pennines and Welsh mountains rising to their brown and grey heights from the green lowlands of the great English rivers. It is too large a map to see the whole of England at once. To see the North closely, you roll up the South as the great map descends like the prophet's tent in the Psalms! It was given to my father by a friend in the Ministry of Agriculture and came from Sifton Praeds. You can see many similar ones at the Royal Geographical Society.

The Troll's Hut has a stone flag floor and a great open fireplace which will burn Sussex oak and, when properly kindled, can give out a great joyous warmth which affects all the hearth and the stone floor so that the whole room glows. My father discussed this old local method of warmth in winter with his friend and neighbour, Mr Wilfrid Blunt, in whose house were also some large open fireplaces for burning wood. But Mr Blunt burnt birch, a fuel consumed sooner than oak but giving out a more immediate warmth and blaze. Mr Blunt's stone floor in his hall was mainly of that beautiful 'Sussex marble'—winkle fossils. It is curious to me that electric or 'central' heating never achieves the glorious glow and comfort of wellbeing which a great oak fire will give you in our dark winter days and nights. I have heard shouts of joy when visitors have come in from the wild weather and seen a great blazing hearth, but the little murmurs of gratitude when they come into a centrally-heated house are not at all the same. Flame seems to convey vitality to us poor mortals.

When Mr Somers Cocks asked all of us children to come to London for the day to see the circus, he and my father met us at Victoria and I was delighted and amazed at H.B.'s top hat. I had not seen him in one before, as he kept it in London at the Artillery Mansions flat. I asked him why he wore it and he said in a loud and happy voice, 'Because I am a fine fellow and go to Parliament among rogues and monsters,' with scornful derision. Whereupon Mr Cocks answered back, and with the laughing and talking a small crowd seemed to gather around us, Cocks and H.B. being apparently quite oblivious of their whereabouts. Peter and Hilary were getting restive and swinging on a milk-can they had discovered, so Mamma suggested we moved on to where the cabs were. I have seldom met anyone who could be so unselfconscious as my father when he was talking to his friends. I have often seen scowling colonels in hotels and restaurants leave the room in twitching rage because of the disturbance he could cause with the mere fun of life or a drink with a friend, and there was always the feeling that he was only passing by. When he had piled us all into a cab with Mamma he smiled and waved goodbye and disappeared in the throng, but Mr Cocks remained to see us into our red plush seats at the circus.

One day my father saw the vicar, Mr Alexander Baker, go by on the first motor-cycle to be seen in Shipley. He was quite intrigued and told Mr Powell how much he would like to try one. So by devious ways one was brought from Horsham for my father to try out—it was on approval and Mamma was full of anxious apprehensions (I rather share her primitive instincts about the dangers of new inventions). However, one sunny afternoon, dressed in his riding trousers, which had elastic bands under the insteps of his boots, corduroy coat and a straw boater, H.B. set off for a trial trip. The motor-bicycle (an early Triumph model) was brought round to the front of the house and in a nudging, awed silence we watched and listened while Mr Powell explained its curious popping powers to H.B. He mounted, sat four square and confident with his feet firmly planted on the granite road, took one last instruction, asked again for the whereabouts of footrests, and, with Mr Powell pushing and running by his side, sailed away round the house by the hall towards the village, calling to Mr Powell for final instructions above the roar and 'pop' of the Triumph. Whereupon with wild and youthful shouts of envious approval we broke our moorings and fled into the road, following with the Carnival spirit! We saw him disappear round the bend towards Red Lane amidst the then so unfamiliar snorting buzz and rattle of the internal combustion engine.

He returned walking and carrying his straw hat in quite a short time. Mamma asked how he had fared, but he seemed to have already forgotten about the motor-bicycle. He said in a casual way, 'Oh! it took me into the ditch just by Capps Bridge—I have left it where it fell and Todman will fetch it back. I do not think I shall buy it or ride it again.'

He was quite right in his judgement about motor-bicycles. They have proved most dangerous, hideously exhausting and lacking in all comfort—but for the motor-car he held a never-failing admiration and often used it. Some years before he owned his own motor-car he was the most frequent applicant for the first Horsham Railway Station taxi, an open Panhard owned by Roberts into which you climbed from the back, as with the pony traps of old. It had a chain drive and lasting cushioned leather upholstery. It grunted and rattled along the dusty flint roads, very much alone in its snorting glory, highly mounted on its springs and an object of distaste to those we passed on horse or bicycle.

When we were invited to stay at Picket Post in the New Forest in the spring of 1910, my father hired the Panhard for us and in we all piled, some of us in Mamma's fur capes, she in her moleskin coat with a lace veil over her hat. We children were in high spirits and pushing and shoving, but I saw how subdued and quietly anxious she was. She never liked motoring as it made her feel a little sick. H.B. was as cheerful and instructive as could be and kept telling us all about what we should see *en route*, darting over to Mr Roberts, who was driving us, and giving him intensive urgent instructions which way to go. He had some maps and 'The Ordnance Survey', and sent us by Guildford and Romsey. He would have dearly liked to come, but there was no room for him, with all of us packed in with Mamma, Edith Rance, the luggage, the rugs, the furs and the stuffed toy animals (which we called 'our children'!) He also said he had a lot of work to finish—but then he always had a lot of work to finish and begin—he was a prodigious, almost fanatical, worker. We jerked away, with happy cries of farewell, and Miss Goldsmith, my father's secretary and our dear friend, stood outside King's Land almost at the salute, intense and sharing Mamma's anxiety!

Away we went into another county. It seemed a long, long journey and after a bit we were stunned into a youthful trance of fatigue from the noise, the wind on our faces and the passing scenery. But we revived with instant joy and delight when we fetched up outside dear Picket Post, as its three storeys and 'gazebo' top appeared on the Lyndhurst road among the yellow gorse, and beyond the forest rolled away towards the blue Solent. We took the house to our hearts—it was one of the happiest of holidays—and Phil Kershaw who lived nearby took us riding and walking and told us all about the gypsies and their cunning thieving ways. He had a vagrant's weakness for them and the freedom in which they had been nurtured, and admired their primitive ways and the saucy eyes beneath battered hats, although he saw through their wheedling lies when the begging began! It was largely due to Phil that I was never frightened of gypsies when I have had to battle with their nonsense stories at King's Land kitchen door, and learnt how to get them to quit before one's patience utterly broke down. I wonder if there are many gypsies left in the New Forest now? Our Sussex ones have almost all disappeared—I seldom encounter any.

Our next Panhard journey was to Worthing in the summer, when our friends and neighbours, the Burrells, asked us for the day to Beach House where they were staying. It was in August, a cloudless day of summer warmth and sunshine. The faithful Panhard arrived long before time covered in white dust churned from the roads—all the flint roads had a layer of chalk on their surface. The journey took about an hour as we chunked along through Dial Post, Washington and over the Downs, leaving behind us a goodly cloud of dust. Findon was a sleepy village at the end of the Downs, and a rural road led past the Tarring crossroads to Broadwater Green, with its church and hamlet. Offington Park was still a gentleman's demesne, secure behind its beautiful flint wall with an unbroken rampart of tall well-kept trees along its northern boundary. We all tumbled out, hot and dusty, at the front door of Beach House and greeted Walter, Joan and Peter Burrell with delight, and away we fled round the great Georgian house and down the long front lawn to the raised terrace, where we feasted our eyes on the cool and glistening sea. Oh, happy day, never to be forgotten! How right it was of H.B. to send us by Panhard. He knew how much we would enjoy it and the memory remains a joy forever. It was not until 1916 that he owned a car. It was a Ford open tourer, tough and ugly—but that is far ahead of my story, and J. B. Morton has described it fully in his memoir.

The first day that motor-driven public taxis appeared on the London streets, 'Uncle' Maurice Baring hired one at once and drove all the way here for the fun and surprise of the jaunt! It was small, red and shiny, with a rather silent cockney driver. Mamma and Papa were delighted and overjoyed to see him and the new machine. We children clamoured for a little ride and asked to go down the Worthing road where our beloved Panhard had taken us on that enchanted summer's day. We enjoyed it but felt it was not quite so commodious or dashing as the Panhard! Needless to say, H.B. returned to London with Maurice Baring in the taxi, singing with joy—he loved the convenience of car travel and discovered it enabled him to fit in even more than was his usual custom. He fitted in more doings and goings-on than any man on earth—it was prodigious—and his friends and family often dropped off from his restless energetic escapades as he went. They fell from sheer exhaustion, like tired flies back into the normal rut of dull mankind, marvelling at his disappearing figure. I see, on re-reading his *Hubert Howard*, how dearly he admired Hubert's physical energy and how, when they were all young at Balliol, they enjoyed for the sheer pleasure of strenuous activity the running and jumping escapades together which Hubert led and organized for them in the flat fields and country-side around the Oxford of sixty years ago.

My father distrusted flying from the very start, although as a boy one of his favourite books was *Travels in the Air* by J. Glaisher, which described adventures in balloons and was filled with remarkable illus-trations. He admired Blériot for flying over the Channel, but I remem-ber him saying with great unease of soul, 'We are now no longer an island.' He only flew once in his life and detested the whole experience. It was late in November 1939, the first winter of the war, and as it was the quickest way home from Paris where he had been on business he was persuaded to join a few people who had chartered a plane.

I know nothing of the cost of a motor of those days (1910–1911) nor the expenses of petrol and general upkeep. I believe there was not much choice of models and I know it was considered a luxury, although many an energetic and lively person with a modest income invested in one in spite of narrow flint roads and complete lack of country roadside petrol stations. All the language was French—'chauffeur', 'garage', 'automobile'—which infers that the French had extensively more motoring before English people gradually took to it.

In about 1923 and 1924, when it had become universal, my father bitterly regretted the number of cars on the roads and said with ironic jest, 'the rich should have passed laws forbidding the tradesman and the poor to own cars!' And when they invaded the Shipley lanes of his parish and passed his house as part of daily life, he minded the new danger and disturbance so profoundly that he asked Mr Powell, the miller, to relinquish his tenancy of the mill because of the trucks and lorry loads of grain etc. which had to pass his study window. It is odd that he did not foresee how soon this would happen. He said with mournful sorrow that a great doom had fallen upon beautiful Sussex, as it had now become the playground of London—but I don't think he ever realized the extent to which that evil has gone. He enjoyed driving to the end, however, although he never cared for great speed, and even in those last few years of his wonderful life when he could go out so seldom, although it fatigued him enormously he enjoyed it and loved to see the Downs again of a clear day or notice the landmarks as of old.

I think it was in 1909 that he brought home a beautifully made American Kodak camera. What wonderfully good lenses those early Kodaks possessed! He took quantities and quantities of photographs, but how seldom were they a clear record of what he wished to take! He was a frightfully bad photographer! I think he was too impatient, perhaps, and always in a hurry—even if in the garden taking snaps of us children you felt he was on campaign and that a long day's march lay ahead. Many of his snaps are a reminder now of how the trees and bushes of King's Land have grown and claimed the garden; for these records of forty years ago are startling, and show what happens if shrubs and trees are not kept under control.

Always on the wing, we used to sense the urgency of getting our silly cats snapped by him as quickly as possible. 'Oh, Papa, please snap me with Tibby!' Then the search for Tibby, the arrival of the Kodak from the study, the wriggling and misery of Tibby and the click of the Kodak with cat and child in one heaving blur of struggle, then my father's approaching boredom as the cat shot into the bushes and we said, 'Oh, please one more—wait while I get him out!'

However, he bought Louis a Brownie box camera of his own and Louis became an excellent photographer, taking great pains and not hurrying. If we were playing round by the mill and my Father arrived with the Kodak we at once began to pose for him, smirking and becoming very self-conscious. Sometimes his mind seemed far away and he seemed hardly to notice us, although the Kodak was pointing at us

143

and going 'click click'. More blurs, alas! for the chemist to develop! But there was always hope, and now and again my father recorded small and priceless incidents. He found it a minor activity and recreation which all helped with the mosaic pattern of his abnormally crowded day. His temperament and ceaseless movement would have been more suited to the modern ciné camera. How it would have delighted him! When he made money from *Land and Water* he bought a really good camera which had to stand on a tripod and with this he was far more successful and took trouble with the groups of friends and relations. But how rare it is to find worthy records photographed by an amateur. Really good photos take a great deal of practice, patience, and knowledge. It seems sometimes that just by chance the amateur catches an enchanted scene or a perfect likeness, and then it is worth all the professionals put together. H.B. talks about this in his essay, the 'Portrait of a Child', where he says:

> In a garden which must I think lie somewhere apart and enclosed you come across the English grass in Summer beneath the shade of a tree. You were running, but your arms were stretched before you in a sort of dance and balance as though you rather belonged to the air and to the growing things around you and above you than to the earth over which you passed. You were three years old. As in jest, this charming vision was recorded by a camera which some guest had with him, a happy accident. . . . It so chanced that your figure, when the picture was printed, shone all around with light.

In some ways he had a photographic memory himself, as certain details remained with him as a deep impression if he had thought them important. It always astonished me how all the pictures he made himself for *Four Men* were drawn and painted from his memory of the Sussex views and buildings. The sepia paintings are almost like photographs taken on a soft cloudy English day, with a mysterious haze over the misty outlook which sometimes a camera can catch.

He knew Sussex so intimately and with such love that he produced these pictures as part of himself. He painted and drew them in the study here; and oddly enough his own mill is charming but grossly inaccurate, as the sweeps are represented much shorter than they are. Not that it matters, as he does not say it is his mill. As a matter of fact, he does not give a description of the illustrations at all in the book, as he wished them to blend in with the script, as it were. I always think that publishers should place an illustration with the page of writing to which it refers. Illustrations just haphazard through a book is like having raisins served separately from the cake you are eating.

The illustrations he painted for *The Pyrenees* have the same quality as those in *Four Men* and in *The Path to Rome*, the only difference being that he had many pencil sketches to help his memory after returning home from these wanderings. He never had drawing or painting lessons except at school, but he had always drawn since a child with great aptitude and his mother taught him always to take a small sketch-book with him when travelling, as she had done. She was talented in a simple Victorian way herself in water-colour painting. I always encouraged my own children to 'go sketching' when the weather permitted. It was one of the few pursuits always possible in the war as we had any number of paint-boxes, old and new, as well as pencils and paper. They used to enjoy it enormously and took their friends also.

The drawings which my father made for *Four Men*, his book about a walk across Sussex, he had framed and we still have some of them. Some have been given away.

I do not think he or Mamma ever collected pictures, but he seemed strong in his likes or dislikes in artistic matters. He greatly admired Gilbert Chesterton's amusing sketches of gentlemen of the Edwardian days—he had them framed occasionally and hung on his walls. He thought that Clare Leighton and Bertha Horning (Mrs Frank Collin) were first-rate etchers and many of Mrs Collin's etchings were framed as well. She also gave him several lessons in etching which he greatly enjoyed. Of the finished ones we have his 'Lion on the run', 'The Windmill,' and his boat the *Nona*—but he took this up more for recreation than anything else and he never really mastered the art.

He was pleased to possess a few oil paintings of his forebears—they were not necessarily good paintings or valuable—but he delighted in lineage and thought it was important to know about your family.

Not that he was vain about knowing his, but he felt it was honourable. When writing and lecturing on the French Revolution at great length in the beginning of the century, he looked up many paintings and engravings of contemporary figures in France, and took great trouble about what illustrations were to appear in his books. One oil painting of Danton appealed very much to him, for he judged it to be authentic from its particular history and the documents of the Danton family attached to it. He had this copied with the permission of Dr Robinet, and a photogravure of it appears in the first edition of *Danton* with most interesting extracts from the letter written by Madame Chapin to Danton's two sons when she gave them the portrait. My father had a copy of this picture hung in his study.

When William Hyde, the artist, illustrated with drawings and paintings his book *The Old Road*, he rejoiced over their excellence and had seven or eight of them in photogravure framed and hung along the corridor upstairs. *The Old Road*, the Pilgrims Way from Winchester to Canterbury, is a remarkable piece of historical and topical writing, and Phil Kershaw went some of the way with him along it. Mr Hyde's illustrations have caught much of the romance and delight of the English landscape, and Hilaire Belloc's relish for the country and little towns.

His singing, which was spontaneous, also had a natural quality, as he had never had lessons. It had a very good range and volume and was always true to the note. He never sang to accompaniment but if there was a chorus he made any friends who were with him sing it with gusto.

It was Christopher Stone who made him record four only of his own songs; and it was a great pity he did not record the 'Chanty of the Nona', which certainly used to be one of his best 'turns' and gave immense pleasure to rooms full of friends.

He never went near concerts without the most disastrous restlessness forcing him to leave at once from boredom. He found so much of his own entertainment from his inexhaustible power of entertaining others. The only times I have seen him quiet and absorbed at someone else's performance was at the Holy Sacrifice of the Mass. At this he would be utterly absorbed and follow each word and action. He recommends it as a perfect way to start the day in his *Path to Rome* where on page 46 of that immortal book, he says:

> Of all the things I have read about St Louis which make me wish I had known him to speak to, nothing seems more delightful than his habit of getting Mass daily whenever he marched down South, but why this should be delightful I cannot tell. Of course there is a grace and influence belonging to such a custom, but it is not of that I am speaking, but of the pleasing sensations of order and accomplishment which attaches to a day one has opened by a Mass; a purely temporal, and, for all I know a carnal feeling, but a source of continual comfort to me. This comfort I ascribe to four causes:
>
> (1) That for half an hour at the opening of the day you are silent and recollected and have to put off cares, interests and passions in the repetition of a familiar action. This must be a great benefit to the body and give it tone.
>
> (2) The Mass is a careful and rapid ritual. Now it is the function of all ritual to relieve the mind of responsibility and initiative and to catch you up into itself, leading your life for you during the time it lasts. In this way you experience a singular repose, after which fallowness . . . one is fitter for action and judgement.
>
> (3) That the surroundings incline you to good and reasonable thoughts, and for the moment deaden the rasp and jar of that busy wickedness which both working in one's self and received from others is the true source of all human miseries. . . .
>
> (4) The most important cause of this satisfaction is that you are doing what the human race has done for thousands of years. This is a matter of such moment that I am astonished people hear of it so little! . . .

It was in the Mass that he, more than anything else, recognized the Transcendental and in It found refreshment and fortifying grace.

The only instrument he ever learnt to manage was the humble tin whistle, upon which he could play 'Pop goes the weasel'! There were certain bits of the great operas which he loved, but I never knew how he discovered them before the gramophone came, since he could never sit through an opera but kept getting up and leaving his seat. He took me to *Faust* and *The Magic Flute* and always managed to be in his seat for the pieces he liked. I was so used to his restlessness that I never bothered at his coming and going, but I tremble to think what miseries the members of the audience near him went through at his perambulations. After all, if you consider it, so much of your good behaviour or mine is largely a matter of self-consciousness. H.B. lived so much in his intellect that he often seemed utterly lacking in a knowledge of what others felt about him. If you told him he would be quite humble and try to understand, but it made him marvel. His dislike of boredom or noise was on such a scale that it could not be borne. He was too humble in his love to tell us we were inferior pigmies, but he must often have been tempted to think so! Once when he was talking to Lord Milner up at New Buildings I heard them discussing the danger of isolation from their fellow human beings owing to superior powers of thinking and reasoning! Lord Milner was home on leave at the time from governing Egypt, where he was endeavouring to help Whitehall with the problems of that country. My father had the greatest opinion of his brains and good sense, and he told me on our way home from New Buildings how much he had enjoyed talking to him. But at that date I was no longer a little girl.

We suffered tortures of confusion ourselves when he would, with utter unconcern, tell strangers to get out of his private pew at West Grinstead Catholic Church. If they demurred, he lifted his thorny blackthorn stick and pointed to the brass plates inscribed 'Belloc'—four of them clearly denoting ownership—then at the now bewildered strangers, making as it were a pass at them to prod them out! I wish I could have enjoyed those incidents in fact as much as I enjoy them now in retrospect. But we never acquired his intellectual power of absorption in the minor scurries to that personal extent of his where he entirely forgot self. The paradox was that it often gave the impression of selfishness, which is exactly what it was not—it was the forgetting of self carried to an incredible degree!

I have roughly gathered, up to this page, about nine years of memories. They are meagre and inadequate because he is not here himself to give you small points about his travels, his ceaseless toil, his boisterous happiness and endless seeking out the companionship of his friends to walk and talk or sail and drink with. But I always noticed how it bored and embarrassed him when people asked him about his doings of the past—he preferred to tell an abstract or funny story or to discuss the world at large. But often without being asked, he would tell us about some small happening in the past, something that came into his mind, and then would abruptly change the subject, teaching us all the time to think and think again. This can be very exhausting, but eventually it enlivens and enriches life.

His great gift of using simple language and plain words always arrested the attention, and if he made use of a somewhat obscure word he emphasized it and sometimes apologized for using it. It was the blending of his energy, tenacity, and ideas which enabled him to accomplish so much. Our tenacity in life should be a development from the obstinacies of childhood! And obstinacy, after all, is only a protection, given us by Providence, against being shoved around.

I never once witnessed him in a defeat. When challenged about ideas he could force his poor opponent into silence and bewildered dizziness or win him over by changing the subject and charming him with new aspects. I soon learnt that people would allow my father to say things that I could not. When once in the presence of a loyal Australian I said something which belittled the British Empire, the Australian rose in his wrath and slaughtered my remark, adding 'I will not take from you what I will take from your Papa!' In other words, the poor man had never dared challenge H.B. Poor old H. G. Wells found it was like arguing with the winds to argue with H.B. in pamphlet controversy, for every time Wells put his nose out H.B. pounced again and wore Wells into silence. But if only Wells had continued a little longer I think H.B. would have become bored and also busy with some other opponent. They were great fun for the academic public, those jousts! Poor old Coulton never felt his controversies and disagreements with H.B. so personally as did Wells. Coulton was so detached, he felt sure of his subject, and he had the solid position of a Don. In fact, he disturbed my father's peace of mind in a completely different way. H.B. was genuinely sorry that he hurt Wells and would have liked to put the personal side to rights, but he felt about Coulton's animosity a complete despair—he knew that the fanatic must be left alone. Old Professor Bury was only just rising to the fight when he died, and H.B. was very gallant and did not cheer his removal from the field.—But that is all so long ago!

While we were at Bognor in 1906 a telegram came to our lodgings telling us that H.B. had been elected to Parliament, and Nannie seemed delighted because in those days it was an honour to be in Parliament. His constituency was South Salford, part of Manchester, and he had been sponsored and financed by Mr Charles Goodwin, who became one of his dearest friends. I think he entered Parliament mainly for publicity because it would help to sell his books, but it was also from his love of debate and, being an historian, all politics had a burning interest for him.

For one who knew the world, he had a curious belief in his fellow men, and this was profoundly shaken by what he found going on among politicians. He had not known how fixed the system was, with its generations of privileges—as yet, he was no angel himself, but he found it impossible to conform to the almost club-like atmosphere of never challenging certain glaring dishonesties. I was far too young to know anything about his immediate reactions, but of course many years later he would, in retrospect, go over some of the past and I gathered that it added greatly to the fullness of his life, although it contributed some bitterness too. He loved debate and discussion but detested argument—and how right he was. He did not make many new friendships from among the politicians he met and wrestled with, but I always thought it greatly deepened his love for George Wyndham. H.B. always looked upon him as a man apart, someone of exceptional honour and gifts.

In 1911 the *Pall Mall Gazette* made him an offer to write articles about Napoleon's retreat from Moscow as there was a centenary of that disaster the following year. He accepted with delight as it meant seeing a new country. When possible, he always went to see the places and how the land lay before writing up campaigns.

We still have some of the postcards he sent to us as he travelled along through Prussia and Poland. He set off in late August so as to be at Borodino by September 7th, the date, the scene, and the season of the battle for Moscow. We were bathing in the river Adur on the morning he left, in spite of an overcast sky and end of summer gloom. I heard

H.B. and Laker discussing the hay-stack (1911)

his call and saw him coming quickly down the field from the mill in his London clothes. Scrambling up the muddy bank, I met him first, dripping, and inquiring; he said, 'Oh, my children, I am just starting for Moscow and have come to say good-bye. Be good while I'm away and obey Mamma and pray for me—I shall send you postcards.'

As he bent to kiss my dishevelled soaking hair a great alarm went through me. I feared I would never see him again—Russia seemed so far away, like the end of the world. As I called to his fast retreating figure 'Good-bye, Papa, good-bye', he turned, waved and, continuing his hurried way through the gate by the mill, disappeared—intent and determined as Napoleon to get from Shipley to Moscow. I cannot recall any memory of his return home, but the articles from the *Pall Mall Gazette* were later enlarged and made into a book—and very good reading it makes—published by Nelson in 1924. I never see it on the shelf in the hall without remembering that gloomy August morning and the cloud around my heart. It was so long ago and I little knew then how the thought of poor Moscow would later cast far greater darkness and foreboding across the skies of life. Our Lady will pray for all.

It took Napoleon three months of travel to get his army and himself from Vienna to Borodino, but my father's journey with leisure and trains took under a week.

Only less than three years later, in the last days of February 1914, a few weeks after beloved Mamma had died, I came into the dining-room at nightfall and there by candlelight my father and dear Maurice Baring were sitting together at the long oak table having a little food and wine. H.B. said, 'Oh darling! here is Uncle Maurice who has come all the way from Russia so as to comfort me.' There was something holy in that meeting; warmth and comfort filled the low room. I kissed Uncle Maurice and, tongue-tied with youth, stole away to leave them in their great Christian feast of Hope and Consolation. I can see it now after forty years as if it was last night. I thought again of Moscow and the overcast sky.

13 *Holidays in France*

IN June 1913, Mamma and Papa took Elizabeth and me to France. It was arranged in May and there was unspeakable agony at the fear of it all being postponed or cancelled, as I simply longed to see France again and racket about in trains, savour the unfamiliar and priceless energy of the French, jolt slowly over cobble-stones in fiacres drawn by aged nags in the little towns, see H.B. wave away the beggars outside the churches and sink into the mysterious gloom and echoing heights of cathedrals. There always appeared to be more coloured glass windows in France than in England. Living entirely in the country made the town life of French holidays seem packed with excitements and novelty.

We went first to Paris, hot and vivacious with her great welcome to travellers. Our hotel was in the Rue Croix des petits Champs. It was heaven for us, with the small windows on to the street so full of life and the great red 'puffs' of eiderdown on the comfortable wooden beds. The next day H.B. took Elizabeth and me out to a late Mass at Notre-Dame. We walked there, following or at times keeping abreast with his eager, hurried stride.

Once inside, the magic of the dark and distant chanting filled me with peace and awe. After Mass my father took us to see the famous statue of Notre-Dame—which all the world knows—and I thought of St Joan of Arc (I don't know why). We asked Papa if we might put up candles at her shrine. As he had the French sous in his pocket he said, 'Of course, my darlings, it's an excellent thing to burn candles at Our Lady's Shrines.' So we put up candles, and I remember I prayed for my brother Louis left in England at school, at Ladycross, Seaford. H.B. remarked upon the beautiful golden lilies which reared upward on each side of the statue, and remarked, 'I wish Mamma and I could have golden lilies for Our Lady at King's Land.' I wonder if they are still there, or if they have been replaced by some other adornment.

We walked round the vast cathedral enchanted and full of learning, but Papa seemed a little bored. He never was a sightseer and had forgotten how often his own Mamma must have taken him as a child to see new wonders and experience different worlds.

We came upon a terrible nineteenth-century tomb, the 'Tombeau du Duc d'Arcourt', which was cut out of various marbles by old Pigalle—and thrilled me! An emaciated form leaned from the coffin asking prayers from old mother d'Arcourt with her draperies and hands clasped in grief. There was also the gruesome figure of Death, his skull half hidden in veiled mystery and his bony hand shaking the hourglass of 'Time is no more'. When we left this beautiful cathedral H.B. bought me a postcard of this appalling group, which was very forbearing of him seeing that he seemed astounded that one so young should be attracted to the morbidities of death. I asked specially for it as we were buying postcards. But the crude taste of youth is at least sincere and sensational, and far removed from the experience of death.

We then went on to pay our respects at the tomb of dear St Geneviève. She lived and worked her wonders so long ago (the late fifth century) that her story is nearly all legend, but ever since her living presence and prayers saved Paris from the barbarians she has been patron of this city. Her tomb is in the Church of St Etienne du Mont, and a very fine church it is. The tomb has a beautiful little shrine-like edifice of its own built for it and richly decorated—almost a little chapel within a side chapel. The casket itself is decorated gilt metal and if you kneel right beside it, to your great thrill there is a special opening in the top where you may put your hand in to touch the ancient stone sarcophagus. Many people were kneeling round praying and I would have liked to stay long, for she was and is always to me a great romance. We had known the beautiful pictures of traditional incidents in her childhood life painted by that great artist Puvis de Chevannes for the immense circular frieze in the Pantheon, which is quite near St Etienne on the same rising ground, and to which H.B. took us next. The beauty of these pictures calmed him, so that at last he did not seem in a hurry, and we lingered with them. And most impressive they were. H.B. told us that this mount was where the Roman soldiers of Clovis had their special look-out when they watched for the invader. He seemed to know every inch of Paris and told us so many things from his store of knowledge. Some years before, in 1900, Arnold had published his remarkable book about Paris—it is not only a history of the city but a living blend of past and present. You can take it up at almost any page, start to read and instantly get caught into another world. The introduction he wrote for the book is its perfect curtain-raiser.

I never tired of sight-seeing, although H.B. was always in a hurry. In the afternoon we used to write an essay for Mamma about what we had seen in the morning, and they still make the most incredibly illiterate reading after forty years. Mamma was not very well so she only came out with us occasionally, but H.B. always knew what to see and how to get there. He seemed to enjoy it all very much and we always took refreshment when thirsty. H.B. used to have a bock and we used to have syrup with soda water, sitting at the little metal tables on the pavements of busy Paris. He took us on to see the exquisite Sainte Chapelle and told us how the good King of France, St Louis, had built it for the crown of thorns which he brought home from the first crusade. As he spoke to us the holy purpose of the building seemed to envelop us and the presence of St Louis enfold us with his justice and good humour, in spite of the crowd which was wandering through and staring at the jewelled glass. Owing to H.B.'s living instruction, a great devotion to St Louis sprang up in my heart, and he is my dear friend in Heaven to this day. It is enlightening that he who bore the burden of an earthly crown and kingship should have been privileged to find and care for the thorn crown of the King of Heaven and Earth. I came away very subdued. I have always thought that H.B. was a born and natural teacher. He had such a power of mental conviction that he could communicate his gathered facts and theories either to an individual or to a listening crowd.

In the tram returning to the hotel my father said he would take us after lunch to see and to ascend the famous Eiffel Tower—he thought we had taken in enough ancient facts and buildings and he had had enough of piety and praying! So up the Eiffel Tower we went in a slow lift, like a cage. The height and enclosure depressed me abominably, but not Elizabeth; and H.B. looked thoroughly miserable also. However, I knew it would be a grand thing to boast about when we returned home. At the top spread the magnificent view of Paris and the woods beyond to the South; and, of all wonders, there was a little posting box, with postcards and stamps to buy. So we bought three and sent them to Louis, Hilary, and Peter. My father could not look over as it always made him feel ill, for although he loved walking through mountains he never climbed them to great heights but enjoyed their lofty noble grandeur from the lower slopes.

Next day we saw the Invalides, and our instruction from H.B. was ruined by an enormous kindly American who collared him at once and started asking questions of the most obscure kind. H.B. bade him good-day and, bowing low and taking off his straw hat, said, 'I have to go now, as I am taking my two little daughters to see Montmartre', and we departed so hurriedly that the American gentleman was unable to follow. Up on the heights of Montmartre the new white Basilique du Sacré Cœur seemed one of the largest buildings I had ever seen, although it did not impress me as much as Notre-Dame. But never have I seen so many votive candles a-twirling and glowing as I did there—hundreds upon hundreds—and forty years later when I went with my two sons there were just as many. My father told me that the building of the Sacré Cœur and its sustenance was a Catholic gesture of reparation for the appalling sacrilegious attack on the Church during the Commune of 1870.

We hurried down the narrow cobbled streets to the trams and were guided by H.B. to the Louvre, where the only exhibit he showed us was the painting of our beautiful grandmamma by her husband, Hilaire Belloc the artist. It was a magnificent picture which filled me with vain pride, and was hung alone on a stone wall near one of the great wide staircases. H.B. did not care for galleries, so we left at once and went to the Luxembourg to see the marble bust of Hilaire Belloc, the man who painted the picture at the Louvre. I warmed to his dear quizzical face, and as he was placed on a pillar of about my height in a quiet corner I stroked his cheek. This beautiful bust has now gone to the Museum at Nantes as that was his native town.

Next day we went by a wonderful little train to see La Celle St Cloud, where my father and Aunt Marie had been born. It was a very hot day and we sat upstairs on the partially covered seats of the little train to Bougival. I had never seen 'double-decker' railway carriages before, nor have I since. It was a delightful experience to rumble slowly along through the Paris suburbs, but a short tunnel we went through seemed alarmingly smoky and it would have been very easy to fall off as the compartments had no windows or doors but only a little cover to keep out sun and rain. If you go to Bougival today you go swiftly in a new electric train which whizzes you along through the enormously expanded suburbs and the lovely wooded country which lies beyond. H.B. read a newspaper most of the way and we were too absorbed with the journey and the novelty of being on a 'carriage roof' to ask questions.

We walked from Bougival station by a dusty narrow road down a hill to a cobbled main street, shaded with chestnut trees, then turned into the Avenue Camille Norman, and there on the right next to a little field with a high poplar tree stood a small house with its shutters closed against the heat. H.B. became a little mournful as he approached it and said, 'This was my grandmother's house where I spent a good deal of my childhood. It is let at the moment to tenants of the rather humbler kind.' We went through the little iron gate across a short pavement, the garden being at the other side of the house on a slope and looking towards the Dutreux's *parc* and *château*. The door was cautiously opened to only a large crack, and a Frenchman's voice asked who was there a little testily! H.B. told him, adding that he had his two little daughters and would deem it a great favour if he could see the house. The door now opened half-way, and there stood a burly Frenchman with his hat on who bowed a little stiffly and looked at us with a good deal of controlled displeasure. He said that his wife was out and, although he offered two thousand apologies, that it was not convenient to show us round. My father replied that he more than understood, and after asking about a few of the people in the village we went away. The door shut firmly and this was followed by the sound of bolts being drawn!

H.B. told us that the French are inhospitable as a nation because they think you are going to get something out of them, but if they invite you to their houses their hospitality is immensely long, conventional, and generous. This we discovered to be true when we arrived at my cousin's house a little farther up the village, where we were expected and greeted with excited smiling warmth. That visit seemed interminable but we were at last allowed out into the garden where, in spite of the heat, we put to good wild use a children's swing and discovered a delightful dog which we roused into a frenzy of energy with a ball. The house had been dark and cool, with refreshment in the form of biscuits and syrup for us and beer for H.B. I remember feeling I was a foreign savage because I found the formal entertainment unendurable. I knew there was something lacking in my 'make-up' not to be able to sit it out with a glassy look upon my face—but H.B. was all sympathy for our request to be excused and allowed into the garden. He knew all about our overflowing energy and the horrors of boredom. On the way home he said French national customs were difficult to ignore and that they were highly civilized, which was to him an excellent thing. I remember a kind of shuddering feeling and an unexpressed preference for a native freedom if civilization meant sitting in cool darkened rooms and talking about unknown interests.

Before we returned to Paris we went into the dark little church, where H.B. showed us the font where he was baptized. We then went to the little graveyard on a hillside deep in summer grass, where at his father's grave H.B. seemed sad and, doffing his straw hat, made a hasty sign of the cross upon himself and said, 'I grew up without a father, which is a great loss to a lad.' Then we hurried away down the cobbled street back to Bougival station and Paris.

Next day we took the train southwards for Viezon as we were making for the Pyrenees and Lourdes. It was a small and unremarkable town, but quiet to sleep in and on the main line to Toulouse. After dinner Papa took us for a little walk in the twilight along the canal, where the local folk were also strolling in the cool of the evening. They looked at us with a good deal of curiosity and conjecture as not many strangers or foreigners come to Viezon. Next day we moved off to Toulouse right away south, in a long hot train journey. I can only remember H.B. taking us next day to see the vast, ancient, deserted Dominican church called l'Église des Jacobins. He told us that it was here in Toulouse that St Dominic had lived and preached in the thirteenth century. Its great edifice cast a huge cool shadow across the street as we rang the bell of the adjoining monastery which was answered by a solemn old lay brother who, at our request, led us through the great echoing emptiness of the deserted monastery to a side door into the church. He and H.B. discussed its history, but I could not understand their French. It was curiously light inside as its stained-glass windows had been looted in the religious wars and plain glass had been inserted in its place. It was then a sad sight—a great empty shell, and most of its endowments confiscated. But I believe it is all in use again now since the gradual and triumphant return of the Dominicans to France. We did not stay long as the lay brother was on the glum side, and but for the great pillars and altar there was little to see. He told H.B. there were only three Dominican fathers in the monastery. I saw my father give him some money for masses as he left, and thank him.

Next day we moved off to Tarbes, a little garrison town, and it was from the train windows looking south that I first saw mountains! Oh, the wonder of it! I had been asleep and on waking found that H.B. and Elizabeth had gone into the corridor. My father called above the roar and rattle of the train, 'Come, my child, and see the Pyrenees. They are magnificent.' And indeed they were—great blue-grey ramparts lying all along the south about fifteen miles away, with all their tops in snow on that boiling June day when the train was suffocating. They were a feast for the eyes in the crystal clear summer weather. I think English children ought to see their own Scottish and Welsh hills first because if they don't they seem to be a poor size after the Alps or Pyrenees. We stayed by the window gazing silent and enraptured. The rest of the landscape seemed flat and dull, and no wonder, with that immense wall of beauty beyond.

Arriving at Tarbes in the evening, I found the mountains hidden by the buildings, although here and there we caught a glimpse of them. We were dirty and exhausted, but H.B. seemed to come to life and told us the meaning of the bugle-calls we heard coming from the enormous barracks. Our hotel seemed very new and cool and clean and lay at the very end of the town on the white dusty road to Pau. After the usual excellent French dinner Elizabeth and I went to bed, but H.B. went off to the barracks, walking faster than usual, to discover what regiments were garrisoned there and to watch them and talk to them as they wandered round the little town in their time off. On the whole, I think he had enjoyed himself as a boy for those ten months in the French Artillery, as he always spoke so highly of their vigour and their humour. He said he learnt to cook at that time and discovered the benefits of hard, drudging, manual work. Some of his experiences there are in his book *The Girondin*, which is mostly fiction woven with memories. He wrote it round about 1909 and it was published in 1912, so that his military service days were nearly twenty years in the past. Next morning there was not much to see in Tarbes except the huge market place, which was also a 'barrack yard'. It was here the townspeople held their famous yearly Mule Fair where folk bought and sold the beasts which are used so much by the peasants in the Pyrenean country. H.B. told us that obviously there were large under-hand dealings in old, discharged military mules. I wished the great fair had been in progress while we were there, but it was deserted except for a few townspeople and some groups of untidy *poilus*.

We were impatient to get off to the Pyrenees and Lourdes, our des-tination, which lies right in the mountain foothills and holds the world-famous Shrine of our dear Lady in its cave by the mountain river Gave outside the town.

It was getting dark when we arrived in Lourdes and the hotel seemed a long bumpy drive from the station. The town was packed with pilgrims from every country, and down in the narrow Rue de la Grotte the little trams went clanging by up and down the hill. The hotel was large, modern, and all lit up, and there was a murmuring buzz of pilgrims coming and going. Madame Soubirous, the owner's wife, was expecting us and we seemed to get a wonderfully warm welcome; we ascended to our delightful rooms which looked to the back and there beyond the open window and balcony you could just see in the fading light the little *château fort* which stands so bravely on its immense rock in the middle of the town like a guarding lion. You could hear the distant fall of the water from the weir built across the Gave many years ago when the townspeople altered its course to make a larger promenade near Our Lady's Cave. Lourdes has a way of taking you to its heart and imparts a feeling as if you had come home. After a rather scanty supper, we all four went down through the big gates nearby to the Grotto. All was quiet and hushed after the busy life of the town. A number of pilgrims were silently praying, and a vast number of burning twinkling candles cast a glowing warmth upon the Grotto and Our Lady's Statue up in the natural niche in the rock. The atmosphere of Holiness and the murmur of the river cast a trance upon me; time seemed to cease and Faith seemed to see beyond this World.

I could have stayed forever, but Mamma was tired and anxious for us to get to bed. When I think of that evening even now the Peace, Security, and Fulfilment come stealing over me yet and flooding into every corner of my soul. How great a gift it is to go to Lourdes as a child and taste the holiness of Our Lady's Presence before life has hurt our powers of receptivity.

Next morning after Mass my father took us into the Grotto, where we bought a candle and gave it to the somewhat grumpy old man in charge of the enormous candle stand; I noticed his old lips were moving in prayer all the time (if he was not telling pilgrims not to light their own candles but to leave that to him. Pilgrims are notoriously disorderly and obstinate, and there were hundreds of candles to be attended to). Then H.B. said he would show us what he considered the only good modern mosaic in the Church of the Rosary, where a picture of each of the fifteen mysteries is depicted on a vast scale. It was the mystery of the Ascension, very impressive indeed, in which Our Lord seems actually to ascend in Majestic Peace as the motionless and sorrowful apostles look on powerless to hold Him. I always pay it a special visit whenever I get to Lourdes. It has a far higher quality of feeling and execution than all the other mosaics. There is a finality about it of the Transcendental which is a paradox considering it is the Ascension which is pictured there.

After this we went into the town for H.B. to buy newspapers and postcards; he also bought us an enormous piece of the most delicious nougat—telling us it was from Montpelier, which was famous for this sweetmeat, and that he knew its flavour and virtues! Then he went to a bijou shop and bought us a beautiful little amethyst cross each. The stones were said to have come from the Pyrenees and to have been locally cut and set. The jewel vender had a long and loud conversation with H.B., both of them extolling the perfection of Pyrenean stones and the glories of the mountains, both saying there were no mountains or beauties to compare with them. They took leave of each other smiling and bowing from the waist without having had the usual quarrel and bargaining over the price!

Except for the morning Mass I think the only devotion of the Pilgrims which my father enjoyed was the torchlight procession at night—the 'Procession en flambeau'. This is indeed a remarkable sight—no one could ever forget it and many would like to go to see it again. After dark at about 8 p.m., thousands and thousands of pilgrims with lighted candles proceed all round the long gardens by the river and back to the vast open space in front of the Rosary Church. This can be watched from the great arms and the stone stairs by which you approach the Basilica built above the Rosary Church. H.B. joined in the singing as he watched—they sing the Lourdes hymn, ending each verse with 'Ave Ave . . . Maria' and when finally the 'Credo' was sung by a great packed mass of pilgrims he seemed delighted and said it was magnificent. It is sung in Latin so that all Catholics will know it.

He was however harassed and depressed by the sight of the sick and crippled unfortunates as they were wheeled or carried by.

On the last morning he took us up the local mountain, the Pic du Jer. We went to its base by a special tram which ran out from the town and went up by the funicular. There was a magnificent view of all the surrounding country: the great mountain peaks beyond to the south, all the wooded splendour of the lower slopes and the valley of the river Gave making way for the tumbling glacial waters from the mountains, and the green and cultivated plain crossed by the white dust road running to the town of Pau, which was out of our sight. He pointed out certain peaks and cols still some miles away in the glories of the range before us. We always took his knowledge for granted. But of course he had acquired a special knowledge of the Pyrenees and had written and illustrated a remarkable book about his climbs and walks among their many peaks and river valleys.

On the third day my father took us to Gabas—a then delectable village high up in the mountains on the way to Spain and only twelve miles from the frontier. We left our heavier luggage at the Lourdes hotel, keeping our rooms as Mamma, Elizabeth, and I were returning to stay another three weeks. We took train for Pau and all the way watched the mountains and never tired of them. H.B. had a map of the district and showed us where we were. He always had a map wherever he went, and if he was not reading a newspaper he would be studying his map. At Pau we changed into the little local train for Eaux Bonnes and began to climb slowly up the valley into an exciting district of real mountains, where the river Gave became a tumbling torrent, cool and enticing to look upon. At Eaux Bonnes when we left the train the air was delightfully fresh and we seemed to have left behind us all the oppressive summer heat. This was a sensation I had never experienced before; it seemed accompanied with a permanent sound of running water, at certain places almost a roar, which never left us day or night while in the mountains. Of course every mountain valley has a river and in many places cascades join the river, tumbling and jumping down the steepest of rocky walls. My father told us that some people hear wicked fairy voices in the torrents sometimes when they are alone at night: and suddenly for us children all the serene rugged beauty around beneath the sunlit summer sky seemed to darken, the mountains frowned and the water scolded and jeered. However, the feeling soon passed, but I hoped I would never be alone at night in the mountains.

He was delighted to see how we loved the mountain scenery and wanted to climb and bathe in the torrent. He said the first thing to buy at Eaux Bonnes, before going up the valley farther to Gabas, was a gourd—a leather bottle for carrying wine. I had never seen one before. He took us to a shop which seemed to sell everything, and a vast choice of gourds hung by the door. We chose one which the vender said was made of goat-skin and which had a beautiful little horn-screw top. H.B. had it filled with wine and at once gave us a lesson on how to drink from a gourd—it has to be held above your face at an incline with the horn opening about four inches from your mouth so that you catch and swallow the spurt of wine as it is falling! No mean feat, I thought, and it was delightful fun learning. But the wine seemed sharp and sour, as English children never really become accustomed to wine during their short holidays in France. It was not until we returned home, filled the gourd with King's Land well water and practised many times that we became adepts. Gourds should have a long leather strap by which you can sling them over your shoulder while walking. All the shepherds, mountain wayfarers, and peasants carry them.

My father went off to the only garage in little Eaux Bonnes and after bargaining hired a large, clumsy, substantial car in which we all set off up the valley. The mountains got higher, the great walls of pine trees gave place to rugged crags of rock, and every now and then the valley widened a little and the torrent tumbled faster and with pools and eddies and white foam went shouting down to Pau, where it widens out into a broad calm river. Having reached Gabas, we found the road and river divided; two valleys ran away, one to the south-east to Spain, and one to the south-west—a rough mountain road to the plateau beneath the great Pic du Midi.

When we stopped at the one and only inn to leave our luggage, the proprietor said he remembered H.B. Our rooms were ready, as we were expected, then we went in the car through a wide valley for twelve miles all along the gradual ascent to the Spanish border. Two grinning Spanish soldiers came up to us at the frontier post, and we got out because we did not wish to take the car into Spain. But with great pride I stood with one foot in each country, which greatly amused H.B. and the soldiers. The road seemed to descend at once into Spain and the country beyond was strangely, noticeably bare and barren—it looked like an uninhabited moonland. Eastward to our left for mile after mile, lay a great range of towering rocks, which my father told us were called the Peaks of Hell. H.B. told us how Spain had defeated Napoleon and how he must have looked back at its curious, rocky barrenness with a certain foreboding about his future campaign.

When you look at Spain from France the contrast is most striking— Spain holds a remote integrity, and a rock-like pride seems to dwell in the granite of her side of the Pyrenean wall, a nameless challenge to let her be herself.

After standing once more with one foot in Spain and one in France, we all returned to the inn at Gabas and the hired motor snorted away down the valley back to Eaux Bonnes. We slept to the music of the torrent.

Next morning in the clear sunlit mountain air my father took us for our first climb. I found how impossible it is to hurry, as all the inclines are much steeper than they look and the air has a thin rare quality.

We slowly went up to the plateau under the great wondrous Pic du Midi, and before leaving the Gave paddled in one of its icy pools. While we dipped our feet and painfully walked over the pebbles, H.B. was cutting a large staff! It was a small birch tree, and I had never seen so powerful a young tree cut with a pocket-knife before. He always carried a really serviceable pocket-knife about with him, but the effort and determination needed to smoothe the ends with it made him pant. We brought this staff back with us all the way to King's Land as I was so impressed with it and, looking at it again yesterday and handling it, I am still amazed at the strength and power necessary to do this with a pocket-knife. He was very proud of it when he noted our genuine admiration, and it has been in his study all these long years since 1913. As he had his Kodak in his pocket, he took some snapshots of us, and I asked him to cheat and tip the camera as I crawled hands and knees on a rock to look as if I was scaling a perilous place. This he did, much to his amusement and my deceitful satisfaction. Then I asked if I could photograph him drinking from the gourd! As usual none of these snaps turned out very well, but they were good enough for our entertainment.

When we reached the grassy plateau at last we had a long rest and I was astonished to find so many lovely flowers up there growing in the beautiful soft grass, which was cropped short by sheep and vividly green after the burnt-up summer fields of the French countryside through which we had passed down to the Pyrenees. There were irises of different colours, gentians large and small, fritillaries white and maroon, and many strange new flowers as well, of exceptional delicacy, high up there under the blue sky and the magnificent glory of the massive Pic du Midi. My father told us that it was the high cool air and the gradual melting of the snow which caused spring flowers to blossom in June. He was not interested in flowers, but was delighted by our happiness.

A shepherd with his dog and small flock began to descend from one of the grassy slopes, and he came slowly towards us while the sheep cropped as they moved. He came up to me with a delighted grin and began to talk quite fast, smiling and nodding, but was utterly incomprehensible. The dog watched the sheep and H.B. tried to understand the shepherd's eager questions. H.B. informed him we were English folk staying at the Gabas inn, offered him a drink of wine from the gourd, and told us that he could not understand one word of his excited talk—it was some local patois or shepherd's language. But he was expert with the gourd, having lived all his life with such things. The sheep were moving on, so we all shook hands and we began to descend to Gabas as the shepherd made slowly off to the other end of the plateau. Down, down we went, leaving the grass and flowers behind to glorify their Creator in silence and solitude, down through the pine trees on to the track again and along the side of the torrent back to the inn, feeling exhausted and happy and utterly satiated with the wonder and beauty of it all. And there outside the inn was a vast cavalcade of strange rough men and mules and a donkey or two with packs and curious saddles! A great deal of drinking and good-humoured shouting was going on. Gourds were being refilled, the mules were being given nose-bags of chaff and corn and some were nosing down to small bundles of dry yellow hay. A fascinating to-do in the dusty road! In the shade of some small trees on benches and tables, Mademoiselle of the inn was dealing out great hunks of curiously coarse bread and local 'saucisson'. I asked my father what it was all about and he said, 'Those, my darling, are brigands! They ply their way across the frontier in the summer season, smuggling as best they can the contraband of Spain and France!' As we left this delightful bevy of brigands for the cool dining-room and deliciously cooked trout, we heard singing break out among the happy outlaws.

Next day we went down the valley, returning by Pau, where H.B. said *au revoir* and went on northwards for home. Mamma took Elizabeth and me back to Lourdes for a very remarkable month, during which we joined in and watched the vivid experiences of countless pilgrims from all over the world, learned how to pray, and stroked the goats which lay quietly on the sidewalk in the road beyond the Grotto with their owner, who would milk them then and there for anyone who brought a mug or jug. I cannot remember any of the usual restrictions of town life at Lourdes.

165

Mamma allowed us much freedom, and I hope we did not abuse it or cause her anxiety. Looking back, it seems to have been a heavenly stay in every sense of the word. There were so few wet days, and cool airs from the mountains came down the valley in the French summer heat. Lourdes has the most perfect rhythm, into which you seem to be called when staying there for any length of time, short or long.

By the middle of July my father returned to take us all home again. Sadly we said good-bye to the dear Soubirous who had looked after us so kindly at their hotel, and to their vast dog Sultan, our noisy boisterous companion in the large formal French garden at the back of the hotel. As the long train chuffed slowly out of the little town we saw the Grotto across the wide Gave twinkling in the daylight, with its thousand eternal golden taper flames. Kneeling down in the corridor alone, I asked Our Lady to let me return again some day, and a great fulfilment possessed my heart; in a few months' time, when our beloved mother died, the memory of Lourdes and its blessed graces of Faith and Hope seemed all part of the pattern of life—loss and gain, sunlight and shadow.

My father took us first to Bordeaux via Pau, where we changed trains and, leaning from the window, said *au revoir* for many hours to the glory and beauty of our divine Pyrenees. Bordeaux was fascinating, a vast city of great wealth with shipping all along the quays. My father took us down in the morning to the quay-side, where we saw piles of great barrels of wine waiting to be shipped all over the world. There were men busy with loaded drays and great strong horses un-loading more barrels, and all the busy travail of maritime commerce was being carried on along the cobble-stones by the river, with great ships lying at anchor, leaving for the open sea, or arriving. It was all most novel and impressive and sank deep into my memory. He told us about the vineyards of the Garonne and Gironde country, the profuse yield of the Médoc claret, the golden glory of Barsac, the wealth of Cognac, and how it went in the ship, some bottled and some in barrels.

He took us to see the great Cathedral of St André where the sailors go to give thanks at the marble shrine of Notre Dame de Bonnes Nouvelles, and where also, he said, the wives of sailors pray for those

166

who go in great ships down the Gironde and out into the mighty seas in uncertain weather.

Next day we went on to Tours by train through the plain and there saw the towering majestic Cathedral of St Gatien, standing with its remarkable twin towers, like a great tiger guarding the broad waters of the Loire. Then on to Paris and home to England, tired but triumphant with all we had seen and accomplished, with H.B. as a most resourceful guide and Mamma's loving supervision.

The rest of the summer of 1913 was a little overcast with the sundry preparations of 'going to school' for Elizabeth and me. Also, my mother was not well, and H.B. seemed preoccupied. However, in spite of all this we seemed to enjoy those weeks before the trunks were packed and our fate was sealed. Our ancient bicycles took us round the lanes; we bathed in the Adur, climbed the trees and went to Knepp for tea, where Cosie Burrell took us on the lake in the boat; and we bathed among the water lilies under her supervision and picnicked in the pleasure grounds.

On September 14th we said good-bye to King's Land and all that it held so dear and, climbing into the dog-cart with Mamma, we went sadly away. Miss Goldsmith and Edie Rance waved goodbye and Hilary and Peter ran after the cart—usually a forbidden pleasure, but permitted today for our consolation.

H.B. met us at Victoria with a large box of chocolates and a waiting taxi. He seemed remarkably cheerful and full of plans and talk. London always exhilarated him. He took us across the Park to Euston and saw us on to the train for Stone, reminding us about changing at Stafford and streaking off to the bookstall to buy a lot of papers for himself and some for us. The dark gloom and bustle of Euston left me stunned, and when H.B. suddenly said, 'Oh, my poor lambs, you are going so far away from us', I did not know whether to smile or weep. The shrill whistle pierced the gloom, and away we went northward into the unknown world of St Dominic's Convent, Stone.

At Stafford it was raining, but as our train drew into Stone station a great clearing appeared in the skies, the sun came out, and there appeared a shimmering rainbow in the heavens right over an impressive collection of brick buildings, with gables and wings, dormer windows in the high roofs, and a clock tower—a most arresting sight. I shall never forget it, for they were the Convent and school of St Dominic, built by the holy and heroic Mother Margaret Hallahan to the greater glory of God soon after Emancipation, at a time when the little that was Catholic in England had hardly recovered from four hundred years of persecution. There was a cab to meet us, and we trundled down the little street to the great porch of the Convent, where the door was opened by a smiling Sister. We were received with love and care— a devotion that has never failed me all my life. But when we bade Mamma farewell within an hour, the storm floods broke and we wept as if our hearts would break. Mamma went back to London and King's Land, and Elizabeth and I felt our way into an unfamiliar world, greatly cheered and guided by Pauline Miller, who appeared radiant and full of fun. Many years later she married James Gunn, the artist. She was to be our fellow traveller at the Convent school for four years.

At the end of term H.B. appeared in a great and glorious hurry to take us home. Sister Mary Lucy regaled him with sherry in the parlour, while we arranged, with minute and emphatic plans, for the trunks to go 'luggage forward' to Southwater next day. Sister Mary Lucy— God rest her dear soul—was a sister of our friend Christopher Stone. She was a talented violinist, and her Strad fiddle was our great joy to look upon. She told us it was greatly insured, and it was wrapped in an exquisitely soft silken piece of material before being put into its blue velvet-lined leather case. Oh, what joy as we hurried to the station with H.B. through the dying winter's day to catch the afternoon train to London—and the perfection was that the other girls did not go home till the next day. When we arrived in London H.B. took us to Garland's Hotel, and after an ecstatic meal and a breathless hurry, we set out for *Henry V*. We were in a dream of delight, and that night we thought the soft beds of Garland's were almost sinfully luxurious after our little hard ones left far away at school. My father seemed deeply preoccupied. I think he was concerned about my mother's health.

Now I am going to end this part of my story, because within a few weeks, on February 2nd, 1914, our beloved Mamma died, and life for H.B., King's Land, and us five children was never the same again. By August of that year the Great War thundered and slaughtered just beyond the Downs over the Channel, and I began to grow up. My father told me that after a great loss and an abiding grief there is always duty and toil left to pull us together and to enable us to start life again. He did his very best for us as far as he could, but without Mamma it must have been an intolerable burden at times. We missed her beyond measure and made up our minds to go on missing her, and we would never accept the guidance or help offered in her place by other kindly people. She had been the queen of our hearts and home, and much will be forgiven us because we loved much.

Louis and Peter (the eldest and the youngest sons) were the first to join her in her New Lands, and now dear Papa has gone to her. One day we shall all be united by God's merciful goodness.

Index

Allison, James Murray, 10

Baker, Rev. Alexander, 139
Balfour, Rt Hon. Arthur, 62
Balfour, Mrs Charlotte, 129
Balfour, Reginald, 129
Baring, The Hon. Maurice, 127, 151
Belloc, Madame Bessie (Bessie Parkes),
    4, 40, 114, 115
Belloc, Miss Elizabeth, 105, 109, 110,
    112, 117, 121, 133
Belloc, Mrs. Elodie (Elodie Hogan),
    7, 10, 117, 168, 169, *et passim*
Belloc, Hilaire (the artist), 4
Belloc, Hilary, 105, 109, 113, 117, 131
Belloc, Louis (father of Hilaire), 4
Belloc, Louis (son of Hilaire), 109,
    113, 121
Belloc, Madame Louise (grand-
    mother of Hilaire), 4
Belloc, Miss Marie (Mrs Lowndes),
    5, 115
Belloc, Peter, 19, 109, 118, 122
Belloc, Mrs Stella, 105
Blunt, Reginald, 118
Blunt, Wilfrid Scawen, 100, 128, 138
Burrell, Lady, 167
Burrell, Miss Joan, 141
Burrell, Peter, 141
Burrell, Walter, 141
Bury, Professor, 150

Carnarvon, Lady, 118
Cecil, Lord Robert, 62
Chesterton, Cecil, 42, 43, 44, 45, 58,
    60, 61, 62, 63, 127, 137
Chesterton, Mrs Frances, 110, 114

Chesterton, Gilbert, 9, 31, 106, 110,
    114, 145
Cocks, Charles Somers, 127, 138
Collin, Mrs Bertha, 145
Coulton, Professor, 26, 149
Creighton-Manvell, 47

Derrick, Thomas, 24
Drewitt, Miss, 111

Elliot, Miss Lettice, 114

Fisher, H. A. L., 128

Goldsmith, Miss Ruby, 125, 129, 140
Goodwin, Charles, 150
Gunn, James, 124

Harding, Aubrey, 127
Hayes, Father, 111
Hogan, Miss Elizabeth, 7, 118
Hogan, Miss Elodie (*see* Belloc,
    Elodie)
Hopkins, Mrs Julia, 120, 122
Howard, The Hon. Hubert, 142
Hyde, William, 146

Isaacs, Godfrey, 51, 52, 53, 54, 59, 62,
    63
Isaacs, Harry, 53
Isaacs, Rt Hon. Rufus, 51, 53, 54, 55,
    56, 59, 60, 63

Jebb, Julian, 104, 105
Jebb, Philip, 105
Joel, Miss Grace, 111
Jowitt, Professor Benjamin, 7